"What a privilege to be a fly on the wall listening to these enriching, wise, insightful conversations. Lisa's book offers a practical, deeply human guide and is an invaluable resource for anyone seeking to lead with authenticity, integrity, and lasting impact."

—*Betsy de Thierry*, Consultant Psychotherapist, Author, and Founder of Trauma Recovery Global and Trauma Recovery Centres

"What I like about this book is the huge wealth of experience that it provides. Each chapter is focused on a different practitioner and rooted in different practice. The book places an emphasis on partnerships across sectors and is easy to dip in and out of for staff CPD. It truly is a welcome addition. Thank you."

—*Andrew Moffat MBE*, CEO of the No Outsiders charity

"This is not a conventional leadership manual, but it is certainly a book every leader should read. The author's motivation—to respond to a period of profound personal and professional upheaval, including a critical illness—adds a deeply human and powerful dimension to the work. This is a book of courage. It stands apart through its storytelling approach and the interviews and personal reflections offer not just insight, but connection. This is a heartfelt offering grounded in lived experience and it is both timely and necessary."

—*Alison Kriel*, Founder of Above & Beyond Education

Conversations that Make a Difference for Practitioners

In this essential book, international trainer and consultant Dr Lisa Cherry engages professionals from education, social work, healthcare, and criminal justice in insightful conversations on a range of vital topics that will make a positive difference for practitioners and their workplaces today.

With integrity and authenticity at its heart, the book explores what compassionate, inclusive leadership really looks like and how to get there. Each discussion brings a new perspective, exploring topics from nurturing belonging and anti-racist practices, to growing from adversity and supportive supervision. Placing an emphasis on learning from lived experience, collaboration, and caring deeply about others, these rich conversations share a range of trauma-informed practices and approaches which work, along with opportunities for the reader to reflect on themselves and their wider community. Children, young people, and their families deserve the best version that adults can be, and each discussion helps all practitioners to understand that the work starts with us.

This practical book is designed for action, for change, and to create something better than we have experienced before. Settings, services, and systems must view themselves as connected communities that have to be well if there is any hope of supporting the people they serve. This book will inspire and encourage leadership teams across sectors to enact a change in culture which makes a difference for all.

Dr Lisa Cherry is a leading international trainer, specialising in assisting professionals working with vulnerable children and families to understand trauma, recovery and resilience. She is the Founder of Trauma Informed Consultancy Services, an organisation which provides a holistic approach to supporting those working in universal, targeted or specialist settings, services and systems. Lisa brings over three decades of working in educational and social care settings and a 35-year journey of recovery in overcoming her own experiences of trauma.

Conversations that Make a Difference Series
Lisa Cherry

Conversations that Make a Difference for Children and Young People
Relationship-Focused Practice from the Frontline

Conversations that Make a Difference for Practitioners
Caring for the People who Care

Conversations that Make a Difference for Practitioners

Caring for the People who Care

Lisa Cherry

Routledge
Taylor & Francis Group
LONDON AND NEW YORK

Designed cover image: Dani Pasteau

First published 2026
by Routledge
4 Park Square, Milton Park, Abingdon, Oxon OX14 4RN

and by Routledge
605 Third Avenue, New York, NY 10158

Routledge is an imprint of the Taylor & Francis Group, an informa business

© 2026 Lisa Cherry

The right of Lisa Cherry to be identified as author of this work has been asserted in accordance with sections 77 and 78 of the Copyright, Designs and Patents Act 1988.

All rights reserved. No part of this book may be reprinted or reproduced or utilised in any form or by any electronic, mechanical, or other means, now known or hereafter invented, including photocopying and recording, or in any information storage or retrieval system, without permission in writing from the publishers.

Trademark notice: Product or corporate names may be trademarks or registered trademarks, and are used only for identification and explanation without intent to infringe.

British Library Cataloguing-in-Publication Data
A catalogue record for this book is available from the British Library

ISBN: 978-1-041-00445-5 (hbk)
ISBN: 978-1-041-00311-3 (pbk)
ISBN: 978-1-003-60935-3 (ebk)

DOI: 10.4324/9781003609353

Typeset in Optima
by Apex CoVantage, LLC

Contents

Foreword	x
Acknowledgements	xii
Disclaimer	xiii
List of Contributors	xiv
Introduction	xx

PART ONE
Leadership   1

  1 **Introduction to Part One**   3

  2 **A Conversation With Emmerline Irving: A Journey Towards a Trauma-informed System**   8
      Reflection   24
      Discussion Points   24

  3 **A Conversation With Carrie Peters: Taking Care of People Who Bring Lived Experiences**   27
      Reflection   37
      Discussion Points   38

  4 **A Conservation With Diana Osagie: Love in Education Leadership**   40
      Reflection   54
      Discussion Points   54

Contents

5 A Conversation With Alexander Kemp: Getting Honest About the Well-being Offer	56
Reflection	*70*
Discussion Points	*70*

PART TWO
Belonging 73

6 Introduction to Part Two	75
Reference	*77*
7 A Conversation With Millie Kerr: The Implications and Need of Anti-Racist Strategic Action Planning	78
Reflection	*98*
Discussion Points	*98*
References	*100*
8 A Conversation With Hira Ali: Recognising and Addressing Islamophobia	101
Reflection	*114*
Discussion Points	*114*
9 A Conversation With Jane Hinchliffe: Decolonising the Workplace	117
Reflection	*135*
Discussion Points	*135*
References	*137*
10 A Conversation With Karen Treisman: Reflecting on Intergenerational and Ancestral Trauma	138
Reflection	*156*
Discussion Points	*156*

PART THREE
Pledge 159

11 Introduction to Part Three	161

12 **A Conversation With Sophie Tales: Harnessing Educators' Lived Experiences of Adversity**   163
   Reflection   174
   Discussion Points   174
   Reference   176

13 **A Conversation With Lou Lebentz: Lessons From Psychotherapy About Trauma**   177
   Reflection   193
   Discussion Points   193
   References   195

14 **A Conversation With Amelia Brunt: A Strengths-based Lens on the Menopause**   196
   Reflection   215
   Discussion Points   215
   References   218

15 **A Conversation With Lisa Lea Weston: Why Supervision Is Essential**   220
   Reflection   240
   Discussion Points   240
   References   242

Epilogue   243
Further Reading   244
Index   247

Foreword

What a privilege to be a fly on the wall listening to these enriching, wise, insightful conversations with professionals who model the model, care deeply for people, and live a life where they are applying the trauma-informed principles into the detail of everyday life in various leadership roles. This is not a book of abstract theories that cannot be implemented in real life, but it is a powerful compilation of conversations with leaders who share raw, honest insights into the application of trauma-informed principles in their leadership roles. It is an outstanding practical guidebook into the real-life application from Lisa and some of her colleagues who represent a rich and diverse range of roles and sectors. Each chapter offers a new perspective from their experience of what it means to be authentically compassionate as they lead and change the culture in their places of influence.

Too often, trauma-informed care is discussed in ways that make it sound like a concept rather than a lived reality. But the heart of this approach is simple: to care deeply for individuals, acknowledging their unique needs and fears, and to develop workplaces and communities where everyone feels seen, valued, and supported. I recognise the voices in this book as not just theorists but as practitioners who have laboured as I have, to create organisational cultures of safety, resilience, and belonging.

The collection of interviews explores the reality of being a resilient leader—one who inspires and supports others while preventing burnout, shaping positive work cultures, and being intentional about facilitating life-transforming human encounters. Themes such as humility, psychological safety, inclusivity, racial trauma, intergenerational trauma, burnout, and belonging are woven together with the lived experiences of leaders who are actively shaping a new way of leading with integrity, compassion, and authenticity.

As a founder and leader of four organisations, all working in different ways to facilitate trauma recovery, I am aware of the level of commitment and detailed application it takes to not just speak about such concepts but commit to a life of continually developing a trauma-informed culture. Sometimes, due to time constraints in conferences, I hear myself speak about this subject without the level of detail that really conveys the degree of time, commitment, cost, passion, and reflection that is required to truly live a life and create work cultures where phrases such as "trauma informed," "emotionally safe," and "a sense of belonging" are not empty words but cultures that people experience deeply before they can use words to describe them. This book explores the journey to create such cultures through commitment, hard work, passion, and genuine care for each individual where the leaders and teams in all organisations recognise their "need to be cared for and loved too." Lisa inspires us with her commitment to lead with deep love and care that does come at a cost. Her book offers a practical, deeply human guide to embedding these principles into everyday leadership. It is an invaluable resource for anyone seeking to lead with authenticity, integrity, and lasting impact.

Betsy de Thierry
Consultant Psychotherapist, Founder of Trauma
Recovery Global and Trauma Recovery Centres.
Author of 9 books on Trauma Recovery.

Acknowledgements

A book like this is only possible because of those who were willing to have a conversation with me that dared to explore an aspect of trauma-informed practice that is often left to the end of the pile: collective care, organisational care, and self-care. All the contributors seek to create systemic change in their practices in their fields of work. My first thanks must therefore go the contributors of this book.

It also feels pertinent to thank those who have cared for me during my cancer treatment and beyond and of course, as always, my beautiful children. Now adults, they continue to travel the journey with me.

Illustrations by Fiona Holiday.

Disclaimer

All those who have taken part in a conversation with me have done so as individuals and not as agents of their workplaces if employed. As such, their views and ideas are not necessarily representative of their place of work.

Contributors

Hira Ali is an inspiring leadership development specialist, executive career coach, and acclaimed writer and speaker. Hira's work has been published in *The Harvard Business Review, Forbes, Telegraph, B.B.C., Harper's Bazaar, Independent, C.B.C., Huff Post,* and *Entrepreneur,* among hundreds of other print, radio, and television outlets. She is a member of the Senior Advisory Team for the Benedictine University Illinois L.E.A.D.S. leadership program for undergraduate women, an IDEA Practitioner at NASA, and an advisory member for the Women in Transport Intersectionality Advisory Group. Founder of Advancing Your Potential and champion of inclusive allyship programs and diverse talent management initiatives, she is also the award-winning author of two transformational books: *Her Way To The Top: A Guide to Smashing the Glass Ceiling* and *Her Allies: A Practical Toolkit to Help Men Lead Through Advocacy.*

Amelia Brunt is a qualified educator, supervisor, and coach. With over 30 years' experience working in education, health, and social care, Amelia has worked, researched, studied, and "lived" to better understand overwhelm, stress, trauma, burnout, and the nervous system. Amelia facilitates training and coaching programmes through her organisation, Well Educated. Her Re-NEW™ framework brings academic knowledge and personal/professional experience together to provide a research-informed and evidence-based approach to personal/professional wellness and effective service delivery. Amelia also works with many clients who report increased experiences of burnout throughout perimenopause and menopause. Well Educated therefore also provides the Re-NEWaL™ programme to support women and people who experience this transition period as problematic and overwhelming. Well Educated works with both individual clients on personal and professional matters of overwhelm, stress, and burnout as well as organisational clients, such as local authorities, virtual schools, schools and multi-academy trusts, charities, and businesses, through a trauma-informed, anti-oppressive, regulated, and relational lens.

Jane Hichcliffe is a community activist in her local area, and until recently ran her own consultancy working with children and families in Leeds, UK using a relational, trauma-informed approach. She has also worked in mental health support (safeguarding) and currently works in the FE sector as the relational practice lead for a large FE organisation. Jane is passionate about relational practice, trauma-informed practice, anti-racism, and decolonisation. In 2021 she was nominated for a Child Friendly Leeds Award for her trauma-informed work with children and families. She has an MA in Race, Education, and De-colonial Thought, and completed research on anti-racist allyship as part of her course. She has a range of experience from different education, public, and third sector settings.

Emmerline Irving is the Head of Improving Population Health at West Yorkshire Health and Care Partnership and has over two decades of experience in public health and community development. Starting her career in 1997 in housing and local government, she became a qualified Youth and Community Worker in 2000 and earned a Postgraduate Diploma in Public Health and Health Promotion in 2007.

Her public health journey began with the Kirklees Public Health Team, where she led portfolios including Sexual Health Services for children and young people. From 2014 to 2018, she was a Quality Improvement Lead at NHS England, improving health outcomes for women, children, and families.

In 2018, Emmerline joined the West Yorkshire Health and Care Partnership, focusing on community health programmes. She also serves as Senior Public Health Lead for the West Yorkshire Violence Reduction Unit, and currently co-leads the West Yorkshire Adversity, Trauma, and Resilience Programme.

Emmerline is dedicated to tackling health inequalities and prevention strategies. She leads efforts to address disparities in health outcomes across different communities, ensuring that prevention and early intervention are at the forefront of public health initiatives.

Alex Kemp is a social worker with 20 years of experience working in the helping professions. He holds a degree in social work and a masters in public administration with distinction. He supports organisations in the helping professions and has particular expertise in governance, coaching leaders, supporting services seeking to be influenced by those with lived experience and change management. He is an approved Department for Education improvement adviser. Alexander has worked in various senior leadership roles within the children's social care sector, including as Assistant Director at Cafcass and as Her Majesty's Inspector of social care in England. He is a doctoral researcher at the Department of Education at the University of York, where he is engaged in a research project associated with the experiences of care experienced people in higher education. Alexander is care experienced.

Millie Kerr is a registered social worker with over 30 years' experience within the profession, 20 of which have been as a manager and senior leader. She has held roles within local authority children's services, adult services, and the charity sector. Millie has worked in areas of child protection, HIV, managing child asylum, child trafficking, care leavers, and specialist FGM services. She has expertise in engaging multi-agency partners, leadership, change management, and delivering training through an intersectional lens within social care and more widely. Millie is a strategic anti-racist lead for Brighton & Hove City Council, supporting anti-racist strategic action planning and culture change across children's services. Her ongoing career objective is to enhance anti-racist practice, and racial and social justice nationally. Millie is also a member of BASW's Children and Families Thematic group and the Racial Justice Family Network, chaired by Coram Baaf.

Lou Lebentz is Founder of The Voyage®, an International Trainer, Trauma Clinician, Award Winning Psychotherapist, and Speaker and Campaigner.

Lou is a highly experienced clinician and well-known leader in the field of trauma. Her background for over two decades was as a psychotherapist and addictions specialist, 10 years of which were spent at a well-known London rehab, The Priory.

Since then, Lou has written and created "The Voyage®," a revolutionary online trauma training programme and methodology for clinicians, clinics, and the general public.

Lou has an eclectic background and fascinating personal story and she integrates many modalities and concepts in her work, from mind, body, and soul wisdom to Eastern to Western philosophies and methods.

These days Lou would describe herself as a hybrid practitioner lying somewhere between being a trauma therapist, a transformational speaker, an online trainer, and seminar leader.

Diana Osagie has 22 years' experience leading secondary education, including headship in a London secondary school and subsequently as an executive head. Diana works at the cutting edge of leadership development. She is resilient and skilled in urban leadership under challenging circumstances. Diana couples sound strategic vision with giving clear operational direction. Diana was a school lead inspector for 9 years with developed expertise scrutinising operational systems and leadership competency.

She founded The Academy of Women's Leadership, specialising in supporting women to grow the leadership cultures of their organisations and to flourish as supremely confident leaders.

Diana has written four books on leadership, focusing on the truth of leading others with humour, love, and strength.

Carrie Peters is Director of Operations for Ingeus Justice Services. Her role includes leadership of Commissioned Rehabilitative Services (CRS) as well as the CFO 3 and Activity Hub programmes. These services are delivered across a number of regions in the UK, from Newcastle to the Isle of Wight, and provide a range of interventions to support people on probation and in custody. She has worked in and around probation services for 29 years, holding senior leadership roles in Leicestershire and Rutland Probation Trust and across two Community Rehabilitation Companies for the Reducing Reoffending Partnership, before joining Ingeus UK in June 2021.

Carrie is passionate about developing and leading transformational services that are informed by lived experience. She is committed to working collaboratively with partners, commissioners, colleagues, service users, and their families to ensure that the best possible outcomes can be achieved. She believes in creating as many opportunities as possible for people to turn their lives around and achieve their potential, whilst making our communities safer, better, and more inclusive.

Sophie Tales is a teacher living in the UK and presently working as a school-based senior leader. Sophie has lived, professional, and academic knowledge of Adverse Childhood Experience which is shown throughout her work both as an author and as a school senior leader. Sophie has been a leader within specialist and mainstream school settings supporting children from ages 4 to 16. Sophie is passionate in her work to support staff and schools in developing their understanding of behaviour as communication, to see adversity in all its forms, and develop strategic relationship-focused school systems to better support disadvantaged families.

Contributors

Karen Treisman is an award winning Highly Specialist Clinical Psychologist, organisational consultant, trainer, author, and trauma specialist who has worked in the National Health System and children's social services for several years. Karen has also worked cross-culturally in both Africa and Asia with groups ranging from former child soldiers, to asylum-seeking young people, to those living with HIV/AIDS, and to survivors of the Rwandan genocide. She also is the bestselling author of several books/workbooks.

Karen has extensive experience in the areas of trauma, adversity, loss, child protection, fostering, adoption, refugee and asylum-seeking contexts, trafficking, and attachment. She works clinically using a range of therapeutic approaches with families, systems, and children in or on the edge of care, unaccompanied asylum-seeking young people, and adopted children. She is also a supervisor, reflective practice facilitator, and trainer.

Karen specialises in and spends more of her time now supporting teams, organisations, and systems. This support is to assist movement towards becoming, culturally, trauma-informed, infused, and responsive. This is at a language, policy, cultural, and practice level. She is an organisational consultant to numerous organisations around the world.

Lisa Lea Weston is the founder and director of Talking Heads Supervision, which provides external supervision and training to senior leaders in Education (pioneering), Care, NHS, and third sectors across the UK. Lisa has been a supervisor for 20 years and retains a small, grounding, drama therapy practice with adolescents which she has been providing for 30 years. She has provided the Quality Assurance to the Education Support Well-being Support for Senior Leaders, Professional Supervision programme across the UK since its inception in 2021. Lisa remains passionate about the impact of supervision on the supervisee, the humans they work with, as well as in how supervision supports work cultures and is published in the arena of supervision supporting Fitness to Practice and its fluctuations.

Introduction

There are some life events that you know are going to stay with you forever. Events such as a relationship breakup, having a child, losing someone close, or receiving a health diagnosis. These events don't stay with you forever necessarily because you remember all of the details of the event or events, but rather because you instinctively knew at the time that your life was never going to be the same again.

As a woman in her mid 50s at the time of writing, I have had my fair share of life-changing events: somewhat unavoidable if you're alive! It is fair to say that I have been through some challenges in more recent times. The period known as perimenopause commenced when I was about 46 years old in 2016. Then, as I was nearing menopause and just starting to enjoy the benefits of being on the other side of perimenopause, COVID-19 arrived in 2020. The global pandemic affected us all in very different ways and ultimately changed how we live. For me, it brought isolation and overwork. It was a hugely busy time in my area of work as I shifted to online work with huge groups of people using technology, and the human soul was ill equipped to perform *all* work in this way. Having been used to travelling all over the country and sometimes internationally, my home was simply a calm and comfortable resting place. Being isolated in the house I had chosen due to cost and being central to the road system, I came to realise that I knew virtually no one and the community was not a place where I felt I belonged. This led to me moving back to the town where I had raised my children.

After a busy year building my new business model, which meant that my work wasn't just about me anymore but now had associates

Introduction

and employees, I found myself in a hospital waiting room, having been fast-tracked by my GP to see a specialist. As far as I was concerned, I was living my best life. I had the stamina to run a business, travel, go to the gym four times a week, manage all my family relationships, *and* I was living near my friends again. In hindsight, I was in the best possible position to deal with what was to come. I was healthy and I was happy.

The first sign for me that something was wrong was indicated in my mental health. At the time I was also in a position, for the first time, to provide myself with some critical illness cover. An independent doctor visited me as part of the application and told my GP that there was an anomaly in my blood results which needed investigation before they could approve my application. Subsequently, she said they were being overzealous, but that we'd keep an eye on it. Mentally, I'd also noticed that I was struggling with overwhelm. My mental and emotional stamina was less robust! This led me to have two panic attacks in public places. Alone, this experience and the blood test anomaly were not enough for me to make the quantum leap to an investigation with the GP, but then came the bone pain. A&E had no idea why I was in so much pain. I could barely walk but they decided that maybe it was a urinary tract infection, gave me some antibiotics, and suggested a blood test with my GP once the antibiotics were finished.

The very next day after the blood test, I received a phone call from my GP saying that I was being fast tracked for further investigation to Haematology and Oncology at the Churchill, the cancer hospital. A blood cancer called Multiple Myeloma was suspected. If I could write a description of how I felt, it was like the world stood still for several moments, without noise, without movement, stillness. Shock. On the 28th November 2023, I was diagnosed with Multiple Myeloma with the consultant, somewhat clumsily, stating that it was incurable but treatable. All I could think about was death. Suffice it to say, there was no approval of critical illness cover!

*

Introduction

This life-changing event inspired the book you are holding in your hands because in line with understanding that nothing was ever going to be the same again, I also had to navigate how I was going to work. There were two vital aspects of this that I need to make clear: one aspect is that like most of us, I have not been blessed with the financial means to not work; the second aspect is that my work is everything to me. My work is my passion, my heart's work, and I quickly realised that without it, I would lose interest in living very quickly. Work for me is an expression of creativity and system-changing activism rather than something I need to do and then retire from. However, paying the bills is an important element of this joy. I'm simply blessed that by doing what I love and feel compelled to do, I rarely see it as work.

Entering 2024 with a year of chemotherapy, fatigue, and a stem cell transplant ahead of me, while being confronted with what all that life meant to me, felt incredibly overwhelming. How I navigated my work through this time led me to think about how we care for the people who care. Having spent many years offering workshops, keynotes, and learning around vicarious trauma, collective care, and self-care, I was now able to think about this more deeply and notice what I personally needed, what helped, and what hindered. This was in part due to the fact that even though I am self-employed, I have many clients and how they did or did not respond to me gave me a lot of insight that I previously did not have. I was able to work on and off throughout my treatments which ensured that my mental health did not deteriorate. If I had been employed, I might well have had sick pay but I would not have been able to continue with my work. I was not sick for a period of time and then returned to work, as the model would be in employment. I was sick, I was well, I was sick, I was well . . . repeat and repeat again, for the best part of a year. In fact, having an incurable cancer means that my health needs are ongoing and are only going in one direction.

This led me to consider how would I have been taken care of as an employee? What is in place for someone going through what I've been through? Which further directed me to think about the

Introduction

multitude of complexities that people bring to an organisation that needs to be worked with. More importantly, for people working in sectors that involve requiring a substantial amount of empathy, where exposure to trauma is part of the work and much of the workforce is motivated to make a difference. How does a setting, service, or system do that well?

Following on from *Conversations That Make a Difference to Children and Young People* published in 2021, this book is an addition to that series. Divided into three parts, I want to take you, the reader, on a journey that weaves around various systems, services, and settings. Part One is on *Leadership*. The first chapter is a conversation with Emmerline Irving where we explore system change from the perspective of population health. In Chapter 2 we move into leadership across a service with Carrie Peters and Chapter 3 moves the reader into thinking about a setting with Diana Osagie sharing on her experience as a Head Teacher. Finally, Chapter 4 is a conversation with Alexander Kemp on leadership across the system, a service, and a setting.

Part Two invites us to explore *Belonging* which is opened up in Chapter 5 with Millie Kerr discussing her work on anti-racism across a Local Authority. Hira Ali in Chapter 6 shares her work on Islamophobia. In Chapter 7, Jane Hincliffe talks about her research findings on allyship with this section ending in Chapter 8 with Dr Karen Treisman on intergenerational and transgenerational trauma.

The final section, Part Three, I have titled this *Pledge* as the conversations have clear calls to action. In Chapter 9 Sophie Tales invites us to consider how we support staff with adverse childhood experiences in educational settings. In Chapter 10 Lou Lebentz's call to action is a focus on therapists' approaches to "doing the work" required to deliver therapy. Amelia Brunt reminds us in Chapter 11 how females dominating the caring professions and education are asking us to rethink how we view the menopause, and Lisa Lea Weston, in the final chapter, ensures that there is a deeper understanding of the vital nature of supervision in the workplace.

Introduction

What I have wholeheartedly understood on a much deeper level is simply how much we need to understand that prevention is collaborative, healing is collaborative, and settings, services, and systems must view themselves as connected communities that have to be well if there is any hope of supporting the people that are served by those very settings, services, and systems.

PART ONE
Leadership

1
Introduction to Part One

How does an organisation find its way to being an organisation that supports their people to be regulated enough to do the work? The essential ingredient for any leadership team is to have the awareness to tune firstly into their own bodies, their own central nervous system as individuals, to then consider that for them as a team, leading to a curiosity about the central nervous system of the organisation as a whole. What do I mean by "tuning in" to our central nervous system? I'm referring of course to our universal survival mechanism which, put incredibly simply, receives information to tell us that we are safe. We each have a central nervous system made up of the brain and the spinal cord and within that we have our autonomic system. Stephen Porges' *Polyvagal Theory* (2011) has delivered the greatest understanding of how we regulate our emotional responses and social behaviour and has influenced how we think about trauma recovery hugely.

Once we can tune into our bodies, we learn very quickly when we don't feel safe, are struggling to regulate our emotions, and are in settings that are causing harm. My invitation in considering the role of leadership is to then move on to thinking about what this looks like for the leadership team as a whole, moving on to the organisation

> **Polyvagal Theory**
>
> Polyvagal Theory, developed by Stephen Porges in the 1970s and 1980s, highlights the autonomic nervous system and how the vagus nerve, known as "the wanderer," plays in regulating our health and behaviour. The vagus nerve "wanders" from the brain stem at the base of the head (medulla), down through the lungs, heart, diaphragm, and stomach.
>
> The three key principles of the theory are:
>
> 1. We have three key states: relaxed, mobilised, and immobilised and these states shift depending on how we feel at any given moment.
> 2. We use what Porges calls neuroception to detect safety and danger using our body, scanning other people. Neuroception is affected by our own histories of adversity or safety, meaning our bodies will be more likely to seek to detect danger (hyper-vigilance) with a history of trauma and more likely to seek to detect safety where there has been a history of safety.
> 3. Co-regulation is the mechanism used to calm our reaction to the threat. We seek safety through facial expressions, head movements, and tone of voice referred to as prosody, which lets others know we are open to friendly communication.

as a whole. It is a deliberate move to open up this section with us thinking about our bodies and how we detect safety, because if we are to better understand how we care for each other, we have to start with how we understand and care for ourselves.

*

Introduction to Part One

This book is my second book in the Conversations Series with the first one focused on what makes a difference for children and young people. This book is about you, the practitioner, and what conversations make a difference for you, the person, in your work. Who looks after you, whatever your position, and how you might look after your colleagues are the main explorations of this book.

As you might imagine, writing a book of this nature is an organic experience: a book dependent on who has the capacity to take part, who wants to take part, who feels aligned to the project alongside who feels resonance with my work. In that context when I commence writing a book such as this, I have ideas about what I want the book to look like and a sense of what the chapters might convey. Essentially, however, the finished product is a unique moment in time of bringing together the people and those people's experiences and concerns that land in that moment.

As such, you may find yourself wondering whether there are missing chapters or noticing unheard voices, or experiences unspoken. Inevitably, not all voices can be heard in this book as not every possible situation could be raised. My hope is that, throughout, you are able to consider how you would centre what is relevant to you in *your* space, in *your* setting, in your specific work. No situation or group has been omitted but rather that which has been brought to the fore has been what is relevant for the people who came together at this moment in time.

Starting this book with a section on leadership sharpens the mind in terms of how we consider self- and collective care. Through a trauma-informed lens, organisations need to have an understanding regarding how practitioners may also have experienced trauma. There also needs to be an understanding of the impact upon practitioners when working with services that are driven to make a difference, yet are without the necessary resources to do so which can then lead to vicarious trauma, burnout or moral injury.

Vicarious Trauma	Vicarious trauma stems from the emotional and psychological impact experienced by those who support and empathise with individuals who have experienced trauma. It occurs not from direct exposure to traumatic events, but from the intense emotional engagement and empathetic relationships formed with those who have directly experienced trauma.
Burnout	Psychological burnout is a well-established consequence of prolonged work stress. Burnout can affect anyone but it is especially prevalent among those working in the helping professions.
Moral Injury	Moral distress can occur when practitioners recognise the appropriate action to take but are unable to act accordingly and when people are asked/expected to act in ways that are contrary to their personal and professional values, thereby undermining their sense of personal integrity and authenticity.

In starting with leadership as a titled section, we can consider the leaders we've experienced, the leaders we might find ourselves being, the leaders we want to be. I think it would be a fair assessment to say that there are people who decide and aspire to be in a position deemed to be one of leadership, or certainly to move up hierarchical structures in a very strategic way. However, many of the people I've ever met in those positions found themselves there by accident and on a very steep learning curve. This section focuses less on what went "wrong" with more of a focus on what has gone "right." Some of the writers steer more to *learning* how to be a leader than others, although it's important to note that this section isn't seeking to give you a list of things to do, of strategies to have, of the qualities you

Introduction to Part One

need. Interestingly, even across the four chapters in this section the idea of and the work of "leadership" differs across all the writers.

Emm focuses on leading the work of system-wide change, moving between looking after those in the system, herself, and modelling trauma-informed leadership, in the context of the National Health Service (NHS). Carrie then explores how having lots of those with lived experiences of the criminal justice system working in the organisation changes the way the organisation operates in terms of caring for its workforce. Diana tunes in to her own experiences and how they informed her work as a school leader and how her own health taught her that something needed to change. Finally, Alex reflects on management and leadership, how leaders are all around us, and how difficult it can be to show up fully as yourself, safely.

2
A Conversation With Emmerline Irving
A Journey Towards a Trauma-informed System

In this opening chapter, we discuss the huge task, a 10-year programme between 2020 and 2030, of developing a system across the West Yorkshire Partnership that is trauma informed. That includes five Local Authorities and every service within them. In this chapter we discuss "The Evolution of the Adversity, Trauma, and Resilience Programme: A Journey Towards a Trauma-Informed System."

Lisa   How did you end up as the Head of Improving Population Health and the person leading on the Adversity, Trauma and Resilience Programme in West Yorkshire?

Emm   To understand how I became the lead of the West Yorkshire Adversity Trauma and Resilience (ATR) Programme it is first important to provide the context around the development of the West Yorkshire Improving Population Health Programme.

        When I first joined the Integrated Care System (ICS)—before its transition into an Integrated Care Board

(ICB)—my role was centred on prevention. This focus was a natural extension of my background in youth work, public health, and my passion for supporting families and children. Initially, my work involved "prevention at scale," particularly in areas such as maternity and broader public health initiatives.

When I first stepped into the role, the concept of prevention at scale was narrowly defined. It primarily revolved around specific areas like tobacco control in hospitals, the National Diabetes Prevention Programme and the development of alcohol care teams. The narrow scope of these efforts was not due to a lack of ambition or vision but rather a reflection of the limited capacity available at the time. As I delved deeper into the concept of prevention at scale, it became clear that there was a significant opportunity to broaden this work to address systemic issues, particularly those related to adversity, trauma, and resilience.

From Prevention to a System-wide Approach

The first three months of my role were spent on a listening and discovery exercise. At that time, I was the only person in post, so I dedicated this period to meeting all our Directors of Public Health and other key stakeholders. My goal was to understand their needs, priorities, and aspirations for the programme. I wanted to ensure the scope was broad enough and capable of delivering meaningful impact.

This initial exploration included many conversations with stakeholders across the system, engaging with different audiences, boards, senior leaders; these conversations revealed the importance of aligning the programme with the priorities of our health and care system while also considering the broader determinants of health.

Three months into this process, I was joined by Sarah Smith, who is now my Deputy Director. Sarah was completing her final placement as a Public Health Consultant Registrar, and together, we continued engaging with stakeholders and shaping the programme.

Through this collaborative effort, we developed the framework that would eventually evolve into the Improving Population Health Programme (IPHP). Designed as a system-wide initiative, the IPHP reaches beyond health and care services to actively engage a diverse range of sectors, including the police, housing, and voluntary organisations. These early discussions and joint efforts laid the foundation for what the programme represents today—a comprehensive, integrated approach that aligns with the aspirations of the system. It addresses the urgent needs within health and care services while expanding its scope to include critical areas such as adversity, trauma, and resilience.

Our vision went beyond isolated prevention initiatives, aiming instead to establish a robust system-wide approach that integrates public health with health and care services. This alignment was essential, as health and care form the cornerstone of the partnership. We also recognised the importance of addressing systemic challenges, including inequalities, climate change, health-harming behaviours, and protective factors, to build a programme capable of delivering truly transformative outcomes.

This was a partnership across all sectors; we brought together a board of colleagues that we felt were the right stakeholders to represent the whole system.

During early discussions, a representative from West Yorkshire Police highlighted the strong alignment between public health goals and the objectives of violence reduction partnerships. This connection led to a pivotal meeting between myself, Sarah, and the Director of the West Yorkshire Violence Reduction Partnership. During this meeting, as we explored the public health approach to violence reduction, I jokingly suggested, "Why don't I just come and work with the VRP one day a week?" To my surprise, that idea became a reality. In October 2019, I began my role with the West Yorkshire

A Conversation With Emmerline Irving

Violence Reduction Partnership as a public health lead, focusing on embedding a public health approach to addressing serious violence.

It quickly became evident that this partnership would extend far beyond providing a specialist public health perspective. It evolved into a groundbreaking collaboration between the WY VRP and the West Yorkshire Health and Care Partnership—the first of its kind. This partnership not only explored how a public health approach could address the root causes of violence but also examined how health systems could play a pivotal role in reducing violence. By adopting a systemic perspective, it addressed the interconnected challenges of violence, ill health, poor well-being, and health inequalities. This collaborative insight laid the foundation for the Adversity, Trauma, and Resilience (ATR) Programme.

This journey—from creating the Improving Population Health Programme (IPHP) to forming a partnership with the Violence Reduction Partnership (VRP)—almost mirrored my personal career journey. Starting out as a youth and community worker, I witnessed firsthand the devastating impact that social and economic circumstances could have on the health and well-being of children, young people, and families, as well as the long-term effects on their lives and life expectancy. This experience introduced me to the field of public health, inspiring me to retrain as a public health specialist. It set me on the path to becoming Head of Improving Population Health, where supporting children, young people, and families has remained a steadfast focus of my work.

The Birth of the ATR Programme

The ATR journey began in the early days of the COVID-19 pandemic when several colleagues from different parts of the system approached me to ask if there was any coordinated work on Adverse Childhood Experiences (ACEs). While I knew of pockets of activity across West Yorkshire, there wasn't any system-wide effort addressing this issue.

Having previously worked as a youth worker and as a Children's Public Health commissioner with experience in addressing child sexual exploitation, I understood the critical links between ACEs and serious violence. Recognising the importance of collective action, I facilitated a virtual meeting with around 25 stakeholders to explore what could be achieved together. The discussion highlighted the overwhelming scope of trauma and adversity in the system and the need for a collaborative approach. It became evident that this challenge couldn't be tackled by any single sector or organisation. People travel around the system accessing services and support, so to prevent re-traumatisation of individuals navigating multiple services, a unified and coordinated system response was essential.

Lisa For clarity, when you're talking about the system, you're talking about five local authorities, every sector within those local authorities, and all those who live within it.

Emm Yes! The system includes all sectors—local authorities, health and care, criminal justice, voluntary and community, private sectors—as well as all organisations and everyone who works and lives in West Yorkshire. Representatives from many of these sectors were among the 25 colleagues at the original meeting.

As we discussed tackling such an enormous and complex topic, we realised the need to first build a shared understanding of our goals and the reasons behind them. This meant exploring the evidence base, identifying what was already happening within the system, and securing the support and endorsement of senior leaders to move forward.

Our first major step to achieve this was hosting a knowledge exchange event—a pivotal gathering of experts in the field, practitioners, leaders, and people with lived experience. This event made our case, presented the evidence base, shared good practice, and initiated the development of the West Yorkshire case for change. It was a resounding success, attracting over 1,000 participants across three days. And what happened after the event was the expansion of our initial group of stakeholders from 25 to 150, marking a turning point where we united trauma and adversity expertise with our understanding of the West Yorkshire System and how systems work, partnerships, and public health, and that is how the West Yorkshire story began!

Leadership and Buy-in: The Cornerstones of Success

Lisa   Hearing the beginning of the journey like that and reflecting on where we are now, having this conversation five years later, and it's the learning from that work that's really interesting to me when thinking about how we care for the people who care. So I guess the first question that I wanted to ask you really was how can leaders integrate trauma-informed principles into their leadership approach when we're thinking about fostering a supportive and resilient organisational culture that prioritises the well-being not just of the staff but also keeps the people using the services as the anchor? I think that balance is quite a tension at times.

Emm   Achieving leadership buy-in was critical. We knew that embedding trauma-informed principles across the system would make a difference and that if we could embed this through organisations and our leadership in West Yorkshire then we could make a difference for the people who live and work in West Yorkshire. However, it was not something that was going to be easy, have an immediate impact on financial savings, or be an overnight success.

So the first thing I knew we would have to do was gain support and confidence of our leaders, aligning our approach with existing leadership priorities. For instance, with the ICB Leadership we demonstrated how a trauma-informed perspective could support West Yorkshire's 10 Big Ambitions, address health inequalities, and enhance acute care services.

We had to understand where our leaders were coming from first and then pitch it to them. So as we did with the improving population health program right back in the beginning, using a very similar approach, we went out into the system and by consistently pitching this vision over and over to a variety of strategic boards and meetings, we built a coalition of advocates. Over time, our senior leaders not only embraced the approach but began championing it themselves.

I have to say that in West Yorkshire we were somewhat preaching to the converted as we have been very privileged to have leaders in our system that already advocate for public health approaches and aren't afraid to take informed risks and new ways of working to improve services and ultimately the lives of our population. Their broader understanding of prevention and public health has been instrumental in advancing the ATR agenda.

Modelling Trauma-informed Leadership

Lisa So my next question is how do those senior leaders model taking care of themselves?

Emm That is a tricky question and one I don't think we've fully figured out yet. While the system has made strides in embedding a trauma-informed approach, modelling self-care at the leadership level remains a challenge.

As a senior leader, I am actively trying to address this within my team. I make a point of highlighting in meetings—whether team meetings, directorate meetings, or staff development days—that if we don't role model self-care as leaders, it undermines whatever we say to our teams. For example, I often tell my team, "I don't expect you to work late at night," but if they see me working at 11 o'clock at night, the message they'll internalise is that they, too, need to work at 11 o'clock at night—regardless of what I've told them. That's why we're making a conscious effort to use our own learning about self-care to model healthy behaviours to our teams.

As a directorate, we are increasingly recognising the importance of role-modelling healthy boundaries and ensuring that our actions align with the supportive and resilient organisational culture we advocate for. This was recently evident when I was invited to present on compassionate leadership during our directorate away day. I firmly believe that by openly discussing the importance of boundaries and consistently modelling them in practice, we can begin to foster a cultural shift—not just within our teams, but across the organisation and system.

Lisa And you've been on a journey with that, haven't you? I've certainly seen a shift in you in the time that we've been working together on your boundaries around your time. They are so much better, and you now take holidays without your laptop!

Emm I have, even though this is really hard when you're in a job where you're so passionate and you really enjoy what

	you do. It's not a job. What do they say? If you enjoy what you do, you don't work a day in your life.
Lisa	So true and you know, I also have had to work harder at that. My health gave me a very clear signal to sort that out.
Emm	We've definitely not got it right yet in West Yorkshire. However, if you think about it, we're probably one of the only Integrated Care Boards (ICBs) to have trauma and adversity explicitly embedded in our five-year plan, our 10-year strategy, and all the strategic documents that come out—it's there, and it's not going away. I'm confident that I won't wake up tomorrow and hear from my senior leaders that it's no longer a priority.

That said, I do sometimes feel frustrated by the limited resources and funding for the programme. However, I completely understand that this is due to the broader challenges in the system right now around finance and capacity. So, we're delivering the work in the best way we can—through strong partnership work and collaboration. We're focused on using the limited resources we have as effectively as possible.

I'm trying to shift my perspective from frustration with the difficult circumstances to seeing this as an opportunity. It's a chance to find innovative ways to increase capacity and capability within the system, by combining resources where possible, aligning with other priorities, and making the most of every opportunity to embed trauma-informed approaches. Ultimately, the goal is to make becoming trauma-informed everyone's business. |
| Lisa | This is a slightly confrontational question, really. Do you think that sometimes people can be so absorbed with their own self-care and really take a lot from organisational |

	care that the people that they're serving can sometimes stop being the central focus?
Emm	I mean, yes, absolutely that could happen, but I don't think that's a result of being a trauma-informed organisation. I think that's just a part of humanity. Sometimes we get so caught up in what's happening with ourselves that it can be challenging in different ways to find the capacity to care for others.

Can you be too compassionate? I don't think so. But can it become overwhelming and all-consuming to the point where it has an indirect or detrimental impact on the care you're providing? Yes, absolutely. That's when we need to step back and understand why it's happening.

If someone isn't doing their job, for example, because they're stepping away to take a walk every 10 minutes, then that's a capabilities issue. It's important to understand why they feel the need to do that.

On the other hand, if someone is practising self-care because they're at a breaking point but haven't recognised it themselves, that's where I see it as my job—and the job of other leaders—to step in and recognise when that's happening. That's not easy, but it's essential.

Yes, sometimes there could be intentional misuse of time or resources, but I think that's rare. It's far more likely that there's an underlying reason behind the behaviour, and as leaders, it's our responsibility to address it with compassion and understanding.

Lisa	And I do think when we've got this aspect of being a trauma-informed service system or setting, we understand that it is so much about how we care for the people who care. That is an integral part of that work.

Emm There's definitely something about compassion with boundaries, isn't there? Because boundaries are essential. Everyone needs some form of structure, even within a compassionate approach.

For example, as someone who has managed many staff, some of whom have had personal struggles or histories of adversity, I always strive to manage with compassion. If someone needs to take a day, I will always say, "Take the day." But at the same time, they know there are boundaries. If they don't let me know they're taking the day, then I don't know if they're safe or where they are—and that's where boundaries come in. Compassion doesn't mean a lack of structure; it means ensuring that the structure supports care and safety.

Embedding Trauma-informed Care at All Levels

Lisa So what strategies do you think can be implemented in organisations so that trauma-informed care is embedded at all levels, so that it comes in at policymaking, daily interactions, and what about how we measure the impact of those strategies?

Emm The first step is securing leadership buy-in, and that begins with education and awareness-raising. You need to give leaders a reason to buy in and bring them along on the journey. If you just throw the concept of being trauma-informed at people and say, "This is what you're going to do now," they'll resist—it's overwhelming. But if you approach it differently and say, "We're going to work on how we can care for each other better. We're going to explore how to support people early on, to help them understand what's happening and mitigate harm," it becomes more relatable and achievable.

From there, involve them in shaping what trauma-informed practice will look like within their organisation. Use a strengths-based approach: "You're already doing amazing work. How do we make that even better? How do we grow that so your organisation becomes trauma-informed?" That's where the conversation starts.

Next, you need clear expectations and strong leadership to steer the process. Without leadership, even the best intentions can falter. Someone needs to keep it on the radar so it doesn't lose momentum. As someone put it to me recently, "Health inequalities should be everybody's business—but when it's everybody's business, sometimes it becomes nobody's business." Leadership ensures that trauma-informed care doesn't get lost in the mix.

Collaboration with leadership also helps address barriers. For instance, leaders can help you make this a priority for someone already juggling countless pressing demands. You may see a trauma-informed approach as critical, but they might be focused on keeping services afloat.

Leaders can help you speak the right language to engage others and secure their support.

Once leadership buy-in is in place, the next step is finding champions within the organisation. These champions can amplify the work. In my own organisation, I've seen this in action. People now say, "I'm writing a briefing paper for elected members—can we add a trauma-informed lens to it?" Or, "Em, can you review this to make sure it's trauma-informed?" Over time, they won't need to ask—they'll just do it. But the fact they're asking now shows that the approach is taking root and filtering into policies and practices.

Ultimately, this is about doing *with* people, not *to* them. It's a journey, and it takes time. After five years in West Yorkshire, we don't have it perfect, but I can see the progress. It's becoming second nature, and that's the direction we need to continue moving in.

Lisa But what you *do* have is you have a demonstration of the ripples. The first place you started with was with the ripple from the top and where you've now kind of concluded it's the ripples that go through the organisation and that's where it really cultivates change.

Emm The progress we've made over the past five years demonstrates the power of a collaborative, system-wide approach. From the initial knowledge exchange to the integration of trauma-informed principles into strategic documents and leadership priorities, the ripples of change are evident. As more organisations embrace these principles, the collective impact on the workforce and the communities they serve will continue to grow.

And it's not just within the organisation—it's happening outside as well. For example, the other day, a colleague contacted us about someone in their organisation, a mental health trust. This person, a midwife, needed to complete some work to maintain her professional validation and was really excited about trauma-informed work. They suggested she connect with us to see if there were opportunities to collaborate. Now, she's going to lead some of the maternity work for us, despite being from a different organisation.

If we hadn't put in all the foundational work at the beginning—those times when it felt like we were banging our heads against a brick wall but kept pushing forward—we wouldn't be in a position where different parts of the system are approaching us, wanting to take a leadership role in this work alongside us. It's proof of how perseverance and consistent effort can lead to broader system engagement and collaboration.

Our journey in West Yorkshire is far from over, but the foundation we've built ensures that becoming trauma informed and responsive remains a cornerstone of our system. By caring for the people who care for others, we're fostering a culture of compassion, resilience, and hope for the future.

The Listening Project: Amplifying Voices, Driving Change

Lisa We've been working together since 2021 and one of the projects that we're currently working on now is called The Listening Project. Can you describe it and how it came about?

Emm For me, The Listening Project is an opportunity to truly understand what's happened to someone. It's about putting a human lens on their life story, reflecting on where the system has let them down, where it's done things right, and where it could have done better. The project is about learning from these human journeys—identifying where we could have made a difference and using those insights to inform the changes needed to become a trauma-informed organisation.

It's also about recognising that this work addresses two goals. One is understanding the cost of trauma, which can feel uncomfortable for me because, in an ideal world, it shouldn't matter what it costs the system to help someone—we should just help them, full stop. But in reality, I need to evidence the impact to leaders, policymakers, and funders. That's how we secure the investment needed, whether now or in the future when resources are more available.

At the same time, this project is not just about costs or securing funding. For me, the heart of The Listening Project is understanding the human cost. It's about asking: What's the cost of us not getting this right? How many people are we harming? How many people could we have helped if the system had the right support in place at the right time?

Lisa And we've chosen to do this piece of work with the workforce across the partnership, because we're particularly interested in who works in the Partnership. This supports thinking that trauma and adversity is something that affects us *all* rather than the previous model, the more traditional model, which was very focused on this idea that there was a professional and there was a person using a service. We've really moved mountains in understanding that the professions, the helping professions, are full of human beings who've had experiences too, and actually more likely to be so, because people are often driven by their own experiences into professions that help and support humans.

Emm Absolutely. While the primary focus is the NHS workforce, this is open to all sectors. Of course, we expect the NHS workforce to engage more readily because they're more likely to see our bulletins and emails.

There were two main reasons we started with the workforce. First, it felt safer than going directly to the public, especially when we don't yet have all the necessary services in place to support them. By focusing on staff, we know we can rely on resources like the staff health and well-being hubs. These hubs, which are open to anyone participating in this project, provide an added layer of support.

Second, as you said, the people who work in West Yorkshire's health and care services are the communities and neighbourhoods themselves. If we get it right for our staff, we'll get it right for everyone. Understanding what's happening with our workforce allows us to better support them, which in turn creates a ripple effect that benefits the people they care for.

After all, staff weren't always doctors, nurses, or police officers—they were children who grew up in these communities and within the same systems.

Lisa   From my perspective, it's a lovely project to undertake, to spend time speaking with people, in a very careful and gentle way, supporting people to reflect back and think about what might have happened and where any intervention was, but more importantly from my perspective, where it wasn't.

And it was really good doing the pilot study which we did to test out the methodology of the program and finding out that actually for most people what was missing was being noticed in the school setting.

Emm   I completely agree. The pilot gave us such valuable insights. For example, when five people in the study identified education as an issue, there's clearly something there, isn't there? It highlighted an area for improvement. That alone is something we can take back to the wider system as evidence of where changes are needed.

Another exciting aspect of The Listening Project is its potential to empower other organisations. Our goal is to train them to deliver their own listening projects, embedding this approach as part of their workforce well-being strategies. For example, during a training session with detention officers in Manchester, we discussed how support often comes too late—when staff are already burnt out or after an incident has occurred.

We are working with another organisation, where they have excellent well-being plans in place for staff who are unwell, but why aren't we doing well-being planning earlier, at induction? Why aren't we supporting people from the start, helping them stay well instead of waiting for them to become unwell?

The Listening Project has the potential to change that. By encouraging organisations to adopt this proactive approach, they can better understand their workforce, provide more effective support, and improve productivity. It's not rocket science; when you understand and care for your workforce, everyone benefits.

Reflection

It is no accident that I wanted to open the book with the largest project that I have seen and been personally involved in. Changing an entire system across five Local Authorities is an overwhelming task but Emm has provided the reader with considering what a road map for change might look like. It all started with one-to-one conversations, growing into a large project that has changed the ways that people work forever. May the change continue . . .

Discussion Points

1. **Integrating Trauma-Informed Principles**
   - How can leaders effectively integrate trauma-informed principles into their leadership approach?
   - What strategies can be used to ensure a supportive and resilient organisational culture?

2. **Leadership Buy-In and Education**
   - Why is leadership buy-in crucial for embedding trauma-informed care in organisations?
   - What methods can be used to educate and raise awareness among leaders about the benefits of a trauma-informed approach?
3. **Compassion and Boundaries**
   - How can leaders balance compassion with maintaining necessary boundaries and structure?
   - What are the implications of being overly compassionate or not setting clear boundaries?
4. **Embedding Trauma-Informed Care at All Levels**
   - What strategies can be implemented to ensure that trauma-informed care is embedded at all levels of an organisation, from policy-making to daily interactions?
   - How can the impact of these strategies be measured effectively?
5. **Understanding and Supporting Staff Well-Being**
   - How can organisations better understand and support the well-being of their staff in the helping professions?
   - What role does recognising personal struggles and histories play in managing staff with compassion?
6. **Proactive vs. Reactive Support**
   - Why is it important to provide support to staff proactively rather than reactively?
   - How can organisations implement well-being plans and support mechanisms from the start to prevent burnout and other issues?
7. **The Importance of Champions and Leadership**
   - How can identifying and supporting champions within the organisation help drive the trauma-informed care agenda?

- What role does leadership play in ensuring that trauma-informed care becomes second nature within the organisation?
8. **Support for Helping Professionals**
    - Why is it crucial to recognise that professionals in the helping fields are also affected by trauma and adversity?
    - How can organisations create a culture that supports the well-being of their staff who have personal experiences of trauma?

3
A Conversation With Carrie Peters

Taking Care of People Who Bring Lived Experiences

Leading a large organisation of several hundred staff, where some of the workforce are specifically employed for their lived experiences of the criminal justice system, creates a very different organisation. It is unsurprising that there is a sharp focus on being on a journey to becoming trauma informed and how that focus falls, from the outset, on caring for the people who care.

Lisa How would you describe the work that you currently do?

Carrie Ingeus UK delivers people services across four divisions: Employability, Health, Youth, and Justice. We are connected by our purpose, which is to enable better lives. That is what unites us. And we share this purpose with our wider group of companies, owned by our parent, APM. APM is an Australian company that operates across 11 countries. Everything we do is about enabling better lives and we work with people who are disadvantaged in some way, to help them overcome barriers and achieve their potential.

Lisa And your role in that is?

Carrie My role in that is Director of Justice services, for Ingeus UK. I'm responsible for the justice division. We deliver a whole range of rehabilitative programmes in this division, mainly commissioned by the Ministry of Justice, but we also work with other commissioners and customers too. Through all of these services, we work with people either in the community, in prison, or leaving prison, and we help them to resettle, or move on and make changes in their lives, to move away from offending and achieve a more fulfilling and meaningful future.

Lisa It feels important to say, and to be transparent, I deliver a large part of your training programme around trauma-informed practice and Ingeus is one of my favourite organisations to work with. This is largely, but not exclusively of course, due to a certain aspect of your work for which I have a lot of respect. An area of your work that has been of great interest to me is how you work with employees who have lived experience who come to be employed by you via the peer mentoring programme. Could you explain how the peer mentoring programme works and how people from that programme come to be your employees and what the impact of that is for the workforce?

Carrie Yes, you are talking about our Ingeus Academy which is something I also feel closely connected to and proud to talk about. Our Academy began with our peer mentoring programme, which is something we established many years ago. We brought together the experience and expertise of all the people working in the Ingeus Justice team. Some of these people came from the probation service, and some from other organisations. We used all of this expertise to set up our peer mentoring programme, where we identify opportunities for people who join as a participant of our service to become a mentor and work alongside us. We spot talent, and notice when a person would make a great peer mentor.

So, we ask people, is peer mentoring something you have ever thought about? A lot of people have said to me over the years, that this is quite a defining moment. The moment when somebody has seen their talent, seen their potential and says "Hey, I think you could be really good at this." In desistance terms, it's to do with identity and relabelling, being seen as somebody who can make good, do good, and for them to feel, sometimes for the first time, that they have a positive contribution to make.

So, that's when they would be invited onto our peer mentor training. This is something which we have developed over many years, and it continues to develop, but it's very much a tried and tested programme now, which delivers results.

Lisa What does that training consist of? How does it work?

Carrie Well, the training is delivered over eight weeks. We have Peer Mentor Leads based in all of our regional teams and they carry out the recruitment, the preparation, and the training. The training is delivered in groups and focuses on things like boundaries, diversity and inclusion, motivational interviewing, communication and listening skills, understanding risk, as well of course as confidentiality. We often see very close bonds build between group members, as they learn together and start to think of themselves in a more positive light. As well as providing support to each other, the group becomes a positive new network or friendship group and gives people the strength to move away from more negative influences in their lives.

Lisa   What happens when they've been through that training?

Carrie   Once they've completed the training, they volunteer some of their time, to work alongside our staff. We make sure we don't ask them to do the work of a paid member of staff; everything they do is complementary and enhances the services we provide. They might join groups, or sit alongside people who need extra support in groups, similar to a classroom assistant role. They bring knowledge, wisdom, empathy, hope, and inspiration.

We've always tried to support people to progress using this experience of peer mentoring to enter into employment, because as an organisation, we are huge believers that employment is really important and that it's not just about paying the bills. It's about your whole identity, your self-esteem, your social circle; it brings so many other benefits.

But as well as supporting people to find employment with other organisations, we wanted to be able to support people to be employed by us, if that's what they wanted. And that's why we built the Ingeus Academy, which starts with the peer mentoring programme and from there follows a clear progression route into paid employment. We have introduced a number of roles, within the organisation, that can help someone who maybe hasn't worked for a long time, or maybe not ever, to enter the Ingeus workforce. The idea is that for some, maybe they aren't ready to enter into a full-time, responsible position where they have a full caseload, are expected to be IT savvy, and everything else, you know; sometimes that is too big a step. So we have created these stepping stone roles where people join us, and then we will support them into our more mainstream roles. Of course, some people with convictions are ready to come straight into mainstream roles from the start. And that is supported as well.

We also had to rewrite some of our policies and look at our systems, to ensure the Academy was underpinned by a robust and supportive framework. There was lots of stakeholder engagement, lots of influencing to provide assurance, address any concerns, and get everybody on board with the concept, so that the people we employed through the Academy, they were fully supported by the systems, the culture and the people around them. That is what we call the Ingeus Academy.

Lisa Wonderful. So in that process of having people with lived and sometimes living experiences of the criminal justice system who become employees of Ingeus, a space is opened up for people to be very open about their own lived experiences, for them to be more authentic. Of itself, it can create quite a safe environment and it's one of the great strengths of Ingeus. One of the things that I really love when I come into your organisation is that there is the ability for people to be authentic in a very safe and culturally supported way. That said, I'm sure that raises areas of concern, of adjustment, of care, when thinking about the welfare of employees of Ingeus.

What does a trauma-informed approach to employee care and welfare look like?

Carrie I think there are a number of elements to that question which are important to address separately. Firstly, when you are employing people with lived experience, it is important to recognise how people often feel passionate about the job; they are driven by wanting to give something back and help people who've been where they are. This results in high levels of commitment and empathy, but can also lead to all sorts of issues around oversharing for instance, or finding it really difficult to hold boundaries. If they know someone's really desperate, they might want to be there for them in a way that perhaps, you know, other employees would see as overstepping those boundaries.

So, there are all sorts of issues that we need to support people with, with additional systems for support, with opportunities to talk things over, to offload and to keep themselves safe and well, and make sure they are ready and able to safely support those people accessing our services. Safety is a key element of trauma-informed practice, creating the right culture and making sure it's all underpinned by proper staff development, proper processes, and by policies that can back up the work that you're doing so that everyone is safe to practise.

Secondly, the work we do is going to be triggering for people. It's traumatic. We deal with some really difficult issues day in, day out, working with people who've experienced trauma themselves and also, working with people who have inflicted harm on other people. There will be things that come up for all of us, particularly people who've had a lot of trauma in their own background. That's going to be triggering. So we need to be proactive and make sure that we've got things in place that people can access, and not just wait for people to come to us if they're struggling. We need regular structures in place where people can check in and talk through their approach to their role, and also whether it is impacting on their thoughts and feelings negatively and what they are doing to make sure they stay well. What are their coping mechanisms? What sustains them and helps them to do the job they do?

We make sure that there's regular supervision in place with line managers of course, but on top of that, we offer regular clinical supervision through our sister company, CIC Wellbeing. This is delivered in groups and on a one-to-one basis and supports people by getting them to think about any conversations or ongoing pieces of work that have been difficult, and how has that impacted on them, how have they dealt with it, and how they might have approached it differently. Really, just helping people to process all of that and learn from experience and go on to be a practitioner who can deliver the best service whilst also keeping themselves safe and well.

We also offer everyone a well-being hour which we introduced because we wanted to demonstrate how important it is for everyone to take some time out for themselves. It's about being proactive. It's not waiting for someone to say that they're really desperate for some space here. It's saying every week, have an hour as part of your working week, over and above your lunch breaks, that is just for your well-being and you can use it to practice yoga, to sleep, read, lie in a hammock, or even go for a run. Whatever it is that sustains you, do that for an hour. This encourages people to get into those healthy habits of keeping themselves well, so that they can go on to do the job that they love.

Lisa You've got so many things in place at Ingeus, which has always really impressed me. I wonder, if there are people who think that there is a possibility ever of over-prioritising how we care? This book's called caring for the people who care. I myself reflect upon and am curious about where that boundary is and how we communicate that boundary.

Do you sometimes feel like it's too much or it's not enough? Or that you'd like to do more and how has that played out from your workforce?

Carrie I think I'm always thinking about the balance, and wondering is the balance right? Have we got the support right? Sometimes I think, we provide extra support to people with lived experience because that's the responsible thing to do. But then how does that make people without shared lived experience feel? They may not have lived experience in the criminal justice system, but most people have been through difficult experiences in their life, and why are they not getting the same sort of access to extra support? You've always got to be thinking about, have you got it right? And I think we adapt all the time. We listen to what people are telling us. I always make it really clear that we're a service to help people. We've got a responsibility to do a really good job because these are people who come to us at a really difficult time in their life, it might be the worst time in their life or maybe, their life's been pretty rubbish for a long time, and they've got very little expectations of how things could change. They may be behaving in a way that's really harmful to other people, their children, their partners, or the community in general.

We are part of a system that addresses all of that and helps people to make changes so they can go on to lead a good and meaningful life, where they can achieve their potential and that is not harmful to others. That's our responsibility. Anyone who works with us, that's why they're here. When I go to every induction for every single person who joins the Ingeus Justice team, that's what I say. This is a really serious job that we're doing. It's really important and because of that, we have a responsibility to keep ourselves well, and to make sure we're doing our job to the best of our ability every single day. If we don't feel able to do that, if we don't feel well enough, then we need to take all the support that we can. Ultimately it is about the service users. We always have to keep that in mind.

Lisa — What I really like about that answer is that you're anchoring the people who you're there to support, but you're also being clear that you have a duty to take care of your employees, particularly people who have lived experience of the criminal justice system and that also, you don't have all the answers.

There's something about what the intention is and keeping an eye on that intention and being on a journey with the work of organisational care. I think it's tempting and there will undoubtedly be people reading this book who would really like the answer to some of the questions that arise. But actually, is there an answer? I suspect that there isn't one answer, and it's about our intention, being proactive, and understanding that you're on a journey. So you're continuously revisiting some of these really difficult tensions.

Carrie — I couldn't agree more. The reality is that if we'd had this conversation two years ago, some of my answers would have been slightly different. If we have the conversation in two years' time, they will be different again, because we are always learning.

That's what's great about working with other organisations and partners and listening to them. There's not a day goes by that I don't hear something and think, "I hadn't really thought about it like that. Let me process that. Let me see how we can build that in."

Lisa — Is there anything that I haven't asked you that you would like me to have asked you?

Carrie — I think the key thing to remember is that when people are willing to use their lived experience in their work, that has a power. It has a power to inspire the people we deliver services to, and give them hope, but it also has a power to inspire and help all of us feel as though everything we're doing has a purpose and gives us confidence that people do change. We can look around and see that there's change everywhere. It's visible. We can see it. We can feel it. And this is because we work alongside people who have been through the system and are generous enough to share their experience and how they have changed their lives.

But there's a danger that comes with that; sharing of themselves can be damaging and triggering. It's important to make sure that people have the choice and that they have full control of what they want to share and what they don't want to share. The hope is that they learn that you don't have to keep proving yourself every day.

Lisa That's so important. I think that's the sweet spot, you have to be very skilled to notice. You have to be very careful that as an organisation you don't overidentify with a person's lived experience. You have to ensure that there is room to make sure that people's own skills become at the forefront. I see this a lot: professionals working in children's services who have experience of children's services where their experience of children's services that they had as a child becomes an aspect of their identity that is overidentified as *the* identity. And of course there are the people who have lived experience of the different services who may choose not to be open about their lived experiences for a variety of reasons.

I was thinking as well about stigmatisation.

Carrie	Yes, that is so important. We employ people because of the skills and talent they bring. If they have lived experience which brings with it wisdom, insight, and empathy, then that can very much enhance the way they do their job, but that is not all they bring, and that cannot be the only reason they are employed in the role. I think I know what you mean about stigmatisation too. Long-term desistance requires a change in identity and an acceptance, a moving on from the past and a changed narrative. People should not have to keep telling their stories; their past is their past. It is where they have come from, but it is where they are now, and where they want to be in the future, that is so much more important.
Lisa	Ingeus isn't really well known for this work. If we think about Timpsons, there's quite a lot of knowledge in the public domain about the work that Timpsons do with people who have previous experience of the criminal justice system. Ingeus does this on a very large scale and I love that this book can actually tell everybody about the work that you do.

Reflection

While there are people with all sorts of lived experiences across a workforce, that people are specifically employed *because* of their lived experiences changes the dynamics within an organisation. It makes how people are cared for explicit. It highlights some of the emotional labour involved for individuals when lived experience meets that experience in a work setting. It is ultimately a teacher of exemplary practice in this area.

Discussion Points

1. **Peer Mentoring Programme**
   - What does it mean to truly see the potential in someone, and how can I be more intentional about recognising it?
   - Have I ever experienced a "defining moment" where someone saw potential in me? How did that affect my path?
2. **Purpose and Role**
   - How do I connect with the purpose of my organisation, and how does that purpose guide my daily work?
   - In what ways do my responsibilities contribute to meaningful outcomes for the people we support?
3. **Trauma-Informed Approach**
   - What does a trauma-informed workplace mean to me, and what does it look like in action?
   - What regular supports help me process emotionally difficult aspects of my job? Am I making full use of them?
4. **Finding Balance**
   - How do I personally balance care for myself and others with a strong commitment to the outcomes we are trying to achieve?
   - Are there ways our systems or policies could be more inclusive or adaptable to the needs of staff with different experiences?
5. **Growth and Learning**
   - How has my thinking changed over time about care and support in the workplace—and where might I still need to grow?
   - What role does choice and autonomy play in sharing personal experiences at work, and how can I respect those boundaries in others?

6. **Exploration and Self-Enquiry**
   - In what ways does working alongside people with lived experience inspire or challenge me personally and professionally?
   - What assumptions might I hold about people with criminal justice involvement, and how are those being reshaped through my work?
7. **Creating Safety**
   - How do I contribute to creating a safe and authentic environment for both colleagues and service users?
   - What actions do I take—consciously or unconsciously—to help create a sense of emotional, psychological, or cultural safety for others in my workplace?
8. **Organisational Care**
   - When I think about organisational care, where do I notice tension between emotional support and professional accountability?
   - What does being on a "journey" with organisational care mean to me, and how can I remain open to learning and evolving within it?

4
A Conservation With Diana Osagie

Love in Education Leadership

From the perspective of leading a large inner-city school, Diana talks about system change that focuses on caring for the staff in order that the best possible outcomes are achievable for the children and young people within that setting. Driven by childhood experiences as we often are, Diana attributes to the values of her parents and her own experiences of poverty.

Lisa Tell me how you came to be working in the space of leadership with a lens of thinking about how we care for the people who care.

Diana Well, I think it stems from the foundation of who I am as a person and of my life, because I'm here in this space in a sustained way. I'm not floating through. It's not a stepping stone in my career. It's a space where I dwell rather than I pass through. I choose to live in this space. Love—the action version of the word, the verb aspect of that word. I love that word and what it means or can mean in the workplace. I wasn't able to articulate that in that way in my younger leadership days. I was a secondary head teacher. Before that, I was a deputy head for 10 years. Before that, a head of year and so on. I've always worked on the caring side of school, the pastoral side, the love side of school.

I missed that stage between middle and senior leadership we call assistant head. I missed that stage altogether and I went straight to deputy headship from being a head of year. So, I had to learn how to master relationships.

I made mistakes. I made colossal mistakes because I didn't understand the depth of care, the depth of love that you need to give to people who you work with. If you want the best out of anyone, you have to love them. There's no other way. You can't lead outside the way humanity works.

Humans thrive on love. Because the human works for you, that doesn't change. Oh, I work for that person, therefore I don't need to be loved. When I go home, I'm not paid, therefore love reigns. Love reigns in humanity. It just does. I care deeply for their personal narrative as well as the narrative of the young people that we serve.

I can only be an effective head teacher, an effective leader, if they—my staff—are thriving. Otherwise, I become simply somebody holding the orchestra baton. Music is made but without love. You know when an orchestra has love, humanity, and emotion in it; it's a very different experience to one where you sit there and you think, oh my days—why are they making those squeaking noises?

I need you to love each other because we chose to serve in challenging schools. It was a choice. I could have served anywhere in the world. I was a competent teacher, a competent leader, but I chose the rock face because that suited my skill set. It suited who I am, how I love, how I lead.

The cliche of wanting to make a difference is true. Those children would only get through if we brought our A game. They didn't have private tutors, they didn't have parents (some of them). And so, their society was already set up against them. You know, "children like you" don't do "things" like this. "Things" being have a great career, have a fulfilling life. Children like you get a zero-hour contract in a job that takes you nowhere for minimum pay. We'll even tell you it's minimum wage, so you don't get confused as to where you stand in society, and you'll be happy with that, and whilst you're at school we'll label you pupil premium or disadvantaged, so you really know who you are.

I need teachers, support staff, central team, my PA, I need everyone to stand with me and love enough that we build teams that underpin transformation.

These young people, through the curriculum, through pastoral care systems, through applying for university, all of this takes deep love, because some of these kids don't want to do it. They don't know that the future will be brighter if we get them through education well. Because all they can see is the glory of football, or the glory of Instagram, and those other quick things. I remember they are young and the eyes of young people sometimes value things that disappear in an instant. Quality education in your life remains forever.

So, I need you to love them enough to get them through a narrative that is strongly written, not in their favour. So my staff—that's going to take more than your CPD course, that's going to take more than your master's degree or your diploma. That's going to take some deep love and care. Care on another level. When you're caring for young people, a 15-year-old year 10 boy has just told you to F off, and you're caring deeply for his future narrative, again, you go through our RJ meeting, restorative justice, again, let's try again. You're loving other people's children. People don't see this side of education.

Lisa So, what I'm hearing is that to really perform that work of love, we also need to make sure that the people performing that work of love need to be cared for and loved too. In thinking about loving the people who love, caring for the people who care, when we are loving that deeply there is a cost to us. There's a benefit to us as well, let's be honest, but there is most definitely a cost.

Diana There is a cost. There is a personal cost because when I love you, professionally or personally, I'm vulnerable in your hands. Because that's what you do, you open yourself up, don't you? You share private narratives. You share insights into who you are as a person. When you have my truth in your mouth, I become vulnerable to you, and you can use that against me. Believe you me, my staff tried that one. My first year of headship was an absolute bloody nightmare. Some people who stay with the prevailing opinion because it's easier to be seen to be with the crowd that presents an easier route—than to be saying, "no, that's not right" because people don't understand your motives. In leadership you must lead with clean motives. I may be tackling deep problems, but I do not have nefarious intent—my motives, my hands are clean.

I genuinely want "this" for the young people. I'm not here for the money. I'm paid well; I should be paid well. It's a hard job. But I'm here because I care deeply, and I need you to do the same. Therefore, I cannot accept your mediocrity. I cannot. I cannot accept your self-centred agenda. We, as a school, do not exist for ourselves. We don't. We exist to serve the young people of this locality. Yes, I will pay you well so you can pay your mortgage and look after your family. Of course. Yes, I will build a system where you can thrive. In the school, of course.

I'm not trying to lead outside of the way humanity works, but my motive for doing this may be different to yours and that's where conflict arises, where our motives don't align. Your competency aligns with the job description, but your motives don't align with what, with our mission. When you know my truth, that's where my vulnerability is. But it is also where the steel core is rooted.

Lisa I love how you've articulated that and that's very much my work. I've been engaged in my work for 35 years. You know, I'm not going anywhere. This is my passion. If I was born into money, I'd probably do most of what I do for free anyway.

I'm completely aligned with what I'm doing. So it's lovely to hear you say that and it's raising questions for me about all the people working from that space, with that passion.

Diana If I'm talking about the education system, the way we know that people are working from that space of love is because no matter what the media says, our state education system has never been better.

There are more young people from more walks of life who are successful now than we've ever had, and that level is sustained, I say successful. I don't just mean in terms of exam results, but young people who are thriving, able to take up their place, wherever that might look like, in society after coming through our education system. The number of schools graded good or better has never been higher, the number of pupils classed as NEET has never been lower.

There's more of that now because of the quality of leadership and I think that quality has a big love component in it. I think when I look at how leaders articulate themselves, be it on social media, leaders who other people want to work for, lead more like this.

Does that make sense? Because in teaching, we've never had a shortage of vacancies, right? There's never been a day where there's no teaching jobs out there, you've got to stay where you are. There's always been choice, right? If I don't like the way you lead, if the way you lead doesn't chime with my humanity, let alone my competencies, I'm off.

Lisa We're also talking about values.

Diana Absolutely. I don't have to work for you. And thank goodness, people vote with their feet.

I think where organisations are more stable, turnover is low and when people do leave, it happens for positive reasons and motivations. I think that's because love and care is at the heart of the way people are working and leading.

Lisa You mentioned earlier about how you as a leader took care of your staff, but there was a point of conflict if you felt that the young people and the children stopped being the central anchor to how somebody showed up. Can you speak about that more please because I think that's a challenge for most people in leadership positions.

Diana Again, it goes back to the motivations. I was deputy head for 10 years and a head teacher for six. You inherit the team you've got, or if you come to a new school, you get the team that's there. You can't start with a completely new slate. People come with their baggage. I learned this the hard way, that not everybody is in the profession for the young people.

That is not their central motivation. Many of them, many people are there because it works for their lifestyle. The holidays are good. It's down the road from their house. It's well paid, it works for them. All your mission and values and vision, all of that, they don't give a monkey's. . . . Really, they're not interested.

This is a job. It's not an anointing. It's not a calling. It's the job. "If I could get this lifestyle working in ASDA, scanning the beans, I'd do that"—I feel that is their attitude. Some people think that way. That was hard for me. That was hard for me because I know the consequence of having great teachers in your life.

And I know the consequence of having teachers who don't give a monkey's . . . about you in your life. It is life changing for those young people. So, when that showed up, and it does show up in people, you can only hide your motivations for so long, can't you? It shows up in your work. When it showed up, the steel in Diana would rise, and people would get the sharp end of me, the strong end of me, and that causes conflict, because I will not bow. I will not allow your mediocrity or your bias or your prejudice to influence the potential outcome of the education we are providing here.

When I hear, "well, what do you expect from these children" or, " it is what it is. What do you want me to do?" That kind of attitude, I will not accept it. What I want you to do, I want you to bring your A game. I want you to bring me what it says on your degree. It says that you are a bachelor of science. It says that you're a master of leadership. Bring me that, because that's what I'm paying you for. I'm not paying you for your gossip. I'm not paying you for your Facebook pages.

I'm not paying you for your staff room banter. I'm paying you for your master's in educational leadership—that you sent on your application form. That's the one I'm paying you for. That's the part of your life that I want. I'd love your friendliness and all that stuff, but I'm not paying you for that.

I'm paying you for your masters of whatever it is that you said on the application form. Because that's what I want. That's what I need on behalf of these young people. It's not for myself. I can make money doing lots of things. This is for them. Will they thank me? No, I'm not doing it for their thanks. I'm doing it because I want to genuinely change the narrative that society has written for them.

Lisa So, when you've nurtured that team, how do we prevent burnout and exhaustion?

Diana One, you need a big enough team. Let's just be honest, right? Let's take Julia, a very, very competent woman. She could do a lot of things. But that's not the reason to make her do a lot of things. Does that make sense? Susan, she was a mathematician, a psychologist, great at curriculum. But I don't stretch all her talents across half the school! I need a big enough team.

Two, don't make people do admin that is almost nothing to do with the reason why you employed them. I don't want my head of pastoral care sat there doing data entry. I can pay someone for data entry. When a member of staff says to me "Oh, I didn't get to bed till two o'clock in the morning last night" and I ask "What were you doing?" and he replies "Entering data on attendance" I'd go mad. But it's my fault! I employed him to lead pastoral care across my entire organisation, but he's sat there until two in the morning doing data entry. That's my fault. I take that personally as a rap over my knuckles. No teacher should be doing admin. I employed them for the quality of education and or leadership—not how skilled they are at formatting a spreadsheet.

Three, recognise that you are working with humans. I keep saying it, you can't lead outside the way humans work. Humans need rest, sleep, laughter, fun, relaxation. These things don't change because they work for you. They're still human. The workplace has to have a level of laughter in it. If it's an absolute bore and a chore to work here, and everyone's walking around with a cloud of depression because Diana's going to come around and do another learning walk!

If you make the organisation a place of dread, then you are setting up foundations where people feel anxious, people feel depressed, people can't wait until Friday. You set that up. You cannot plant that and expect roses to grow. You can't. Humans don't work that way. You must ensure that people get to be human in the workplace.

Every single person in the organisation, you must go and make your health appointments and take your mammogram, the cervical smear, your prostate exams. Every one of you, make your appointment this month. Next month is time off time. Everyone gets a morning or afternoon. If you're not intentional about their health and their wealth, you cannot expect them to thrive in your organisation. It is not possible.

I brought in The Credit Union because I had staff asking me for an advance on their wages. They were in all kinds of financial mess, so The Credit Union came in and give them a talk making clear about how to borrow money that was not on a crazy interest rate. If you need, if you need to borrow money, you do it here in The Credit Union, it's safe. As a head teacher, I'm intentional about you.

What's wrong? How are you? . . . I'll be all right.

A Conservation With Diana Osagie

In my office, let's talk—but you're always busy.

Oh, you're right. Sorry, my bad. Tuesdays. Every Tuesday for six years without fail. 3.30–5.30pm head surgery. Ten-minute appointments. You can just go in and make one. You can come and talk to me about anything, on your own, one to one. You can be my cleaner, you can be my deputy, it doesn't matter. I am here every Tuesday. I'm available.

That's when staff disclose to you. "You're not going to believe this, but this has just happened in my life."

I'm thinking, I'm asking you for data. You're telling me your husband's walked out. You're telling me humanity. I'm asking for leadership. Of course, I've got to help your humanity so I can get the leadership bit I need.

Lisa I absolutely love the intentional aspect of what you are talking about. I often think people think that this kind of care happens by accident. Sometimes people make assumptions about what people know. A good example is the one you gave about money and what people may or may not know about it. There's also something about what people might consider as private and what might not be up for discussion, again, money being one of those areas. Talking about things that might be more uncomfortable for some such as health checks and money takes courageous leadership.

But of course, if there is a concern about the central anchor of the work, which is the children and young people, then that changes what is seen as personal or private or not up for discussion.

Diana I think that when you give genuine avenue for people to talk and have dialogue with you, they will take it, and they will disclose sometimes their deepest darkest thoughts. This doesn't mean that in that moment I become their

	solution because I'm a head teacher, I'm not a therapist. But it does mean that I'm able to give them genuine support and signposting.
Lisa	And where do you go? Where do you go for your support?
Diana	Oh, now you see, that's the thing. In the first year, I went nowhere so my health went south. We're going back a little bit now, but when I became head in 2010, coaching wasn't a thing. Genuine coaching is quite a new phenomenon. I knew about it, but supervision in education was unheard of and I wasn't part of a Multi Academy Trust (MAT). My own school was a standalone school.

On July 31st, I had my interview, and bang, I was a head teacher on 1st September. Here were the keys, here's the budget, here's the building, off you go. Looking back, it's dangerous. I didn't have a clue, I had NPQH but no clue.

The NPQH, it turned out, was bloody useless. It was an interesting course, but it had nothing to do with headship. Nothing to do with leading an organisation with a budget of 11 million. What did I know about that? I'm a scientist. I've got a biomedical science degree. What I know about finances is how I run my own bank account. That's it. So where did I go? Nowhere. Until it really got bad. It got difficult when I started having to make redundancies. Ten percent of the workforce being laid off in one year.

I put on weight because I'm not cooking when I get home. I'm doing Deliveroo on the phone. I'm not going to the gym cause I'm up to whatever time of clock doing work. My body began to reflect my level of knowledge, which was that I didn't understand about coaching, I didn't know what therapy was, I didn't know what true group peer alliances were, I didn't have a tribe. It was just me and my body began to reflect it. I was ill, I was overweight, I had varicose veins at the back of my leg, I had eczema. At first, I covered it up; bigger trousers, flatter shoes, I'd put my lipstick on and go for it.

Then one day I thought, I think I need a coach. To me, coaching was the first stage of capability; coaching was required because you're not very good at your job so that someone can say they ticked the box of support. That was in my head. Clearly now I feel differently, but coaching wasn't something that competent people engaged in, in my mind.

I'm competent. I'm not getting involved in that fluffy nonsense. Until one day I realised I needed support. I went online and just typed in "coaches for black women in education." All this stuff popped up and I just went down the list and I just rang a few. Sir William Atkins REF popped up on there, so I just rang him, he picked up the phone and I told him that I needed help. He came to school. He became my coach. He was phenomenal. But that first year scarred me. I was scarred physically because my body went to pot which took years to recover from because I never really got back into fitness for years and in your 40s losing your fitness is more damaging than when you're in your 20s. It's harder to recover it. My heart was scarred because some of my staff became malicious. Nasty. But remember we're dealing with humanity. You can't lead outside of the way humanity works and humans can be malicious.

When people talk about resilient leadership, I think "you haven't got a clue." You are talking from a place of theory unless you've done it, unless you've walked a pathway that demanded resilience from you. Because again, my motivation is young people. I cannot do two months of stress. My school will not stand if the head is off for two months. Remember, we're not a school with a big MAT behind us. There's no one to come flying in. So, I had to learn how to walk in that resilient, demanding place. Whilst wounded, limping, hurting in my heart, and my emotions, what was steadfast was my mind.

Some staff would ask me to relent. To drop the standards, to not go so hard.

You could only ask that because you're already in a place of privilege, because you've already passed, you've got your degree, you've got your nice house, you've got, you know, your life is set up. We've got children living in their car with their dad!

The only way I know that is because I left work late one day and I saw them in the car pulling the duvet over themselves. The next day I talk to the child: "Oh miss, we couldn't find anywhere to park, we don't normally park so close to school." So, when staff are in that place of privilege and demanding rubbish, I get internally angry.

Lisa Where does that anger come from? Is that anger a reflection of any personal life experiences that you've had?

Diana I think so, because I grew up on a council estate in South London. Praise God, I had a mum and a dad, so I had a foundation that lots of my friends envied. We had a poverty of circumstance, but not a poverty of aspiration or expectation. My mum and dad made our council flat a home. We had a dining table, squashed into the kitchen. No space, but my mum insisted that we ate at the dining table. She wouldn't let us eat on our lap in the front room. So we all sat around this tiny table. There's no space but she didn't care. She cooked every day. She worked and she cooked. There was no junk food. I learned to make my bed aged four. I remember going on school journey when I was in primary school, whatever year six was called back then. We were on a school trip. It was paid for because we couldn't afford it and no one could make their bed but me. I remember thinking, what, who's not taught you? We were taught all these things, but we were poor. I wore my mum's shoes to school, got bullied mercilessly because we couldn't afford to have shoes of our own.

I wore my mum's shoes for daytime to school and when it was PE I borrowed my dad's trainers. You know, when I was young, before my brother and sister came along, we would have rice with butter for dinner.

Rice and butter was a bit of a staple. My mum would boil an egg, cut it into four, we would have a quarter of an egg each with the rice, you know, that kind of thing. But there was always a fruit bowl. You know, there might be one bit of fruit in it, but there was a fruit bowl.

So, I had a poverty of circumstance, but I had education. I had a school. I mean, I had to have free transport to get there because we couldn't afford that. I had a free school uniform back in the days of Inner London Education Authority (ILEA). We had our free school uniform vouchers from them. I had school and I thrived, and I loved it. My world was opened through history and geography and all these subjects and textiles. And I learned to sew and to knit and to do science and English.

I lapped it up not because I knew it was my way out of poverty, but because my parents did. So even when it snowed, and I mean it was like a foot of snow, my mum sent me to school. So, there was no buses. School was five miles away. I started walking. And halfway through from Camberwell to Dulwich, I met some other people who said school was shut. I had to walk all the way back again.

My dad sent me to school when I had chicken pox. Little bubbles on my skin. Don't care. Go to school. The school sent me back. The school was everything. For my parents, their school, education was everything.

Lisa And I think this circles us really neatly back to where we started, which was love. I think that's a beautiful place to end.

Reflection

Diana talks about love throughout: love from her parents, love of her work, love towards her staff, the love she wanted her staff to have for the work, and ultimately the love she needed to exercise for herself so she could meet her own needs when her body was telling her that she wasn't doing that. The model being modelled here is one of love.

Discussion Points

1. **Motivations and Values**
   - How do I recognise when someone's values or motivations are misaligned with our shared purpose?
   - What part of my own story fuels my passion for serving others?
2. **Professional Love and Caring in Leadership**
   - In what ways do I bring love, as a verb, into how I lead and support others?
   - How do I model care for the people who care for others? What does "loving leadership" look like in my daily practice?

3. **Creating Cultures of Safety and Belonging**
    - What systems or practices do I have in place to ensure people feel heard and supported, regardless of their role?
    - How do I balance expectations and accountability with compassion and care?
4. **Holding High Standards with Compassion**
    - When I challenge others, is it clear that my intent is rooted in love and justice?
    - How do I navigate the tension between organisational standards and individual well-being?
5. **Vulnerability in Leadership**:
    - What practical steps have I taken to prevent burnout in my team?
    - How do I model boundaries, rest, and sustainable leadership for those I lead?
6. **My Own Support and Sustainability**
    - Where do I go for support—emotionally, professionally, and spiritually?
    - What systems do I have in place to sustain myself?
7. **Leading Through Vulnerability**
    - How comfortable am I with being vulnerable as a leader, and how does that shape the culture of my team?
    - What risks am I willing to take emotionally to build trust and authentic connection in my workplace?
8. **Equity, Privilege, and Perspective**
    - How does my own background or privilege influence the way I see the needs of those I serve and lead?
    - How do I remain alert to—and actively challenge—the subtle ways in which bias or lowered expectations can show up in systems and people?

5
A Conversation With Alexander Kemp

Getting Honest About the Well-being Offer

In the final chapter in this section, I find myself in a conversation where there is an invitation to get honest about the well-being offer, how we can improve staff retention, and the potential for being a manager *and* a leader.

Lisa   So, what role do you find yourself in currently, and how did you get there?

Alex   Like many parts of my career, that is surprisingly difficult to define, and I'll try and explain why. I'm currently working independently with a range of organisations that are in the helping professions and I support and guide them to improve the way that they deliver and provide services to vulnerable families and their children. I suppose you could describe me as a "former inspector, former social work senior manager, lived experience professional, doctoral researcher"!

After a long career primarily in social work, and also as a care-experienced person, I have always been motivated to improve the way in which organisations, but also people, help those at times in their lives that are pivotal. My career in social work was preceded by some other work in the helping professions.

My first job was in a LGBT+ homelessness charity and after my social work training, I worked as a social worker with children and families. I was a manager of social workers. I was an independent reviewing officer. I was a chair of child protection conferences. I was a service manager, a head of service, and an assistant director.

I worked for the largest employer of social workers in England, called Children and Family Court Advisory and Support Service, better known as Cafcass. They provide support to families who are facing scrutiny by the family court, either as a result of parental separation and disputes about what should happen to children when parents are separated, or as a result of the most serious child protection cases where the state is seeking to remove children.

In that role I was responsible for the work of around 300 social workers in a large part of England alongside holding national strategic responsibilities and after that I worked for two years as Her Majesty's Inspector of Children's Social Care in England.

Following that career I was motivated to take a step back from operational management and reflect on the kindness that exists within organisations and provide to the families they serve, and also the staff they have.

Lisa This book is very much about how we care for the people who care and how we do that in the best possible way. With your experience you're very well placed to answer questions about that. How do we take care of so many different humans who are working with trauma? And how do we do that well? What is the best practice? And you've described positions that mean that you will have had exposure to different organisations and hundreds of people. And now in your current work, where you're working with an organisation, you're also seeing around you what works and what doesn't. Being someone who also works with many organisations, I'm very aware that we can tell very quickly when we enter into that organisation whether the staff are cared for or not.

In your experience, what have you seen that gives you a clear indicator or clear indicators that the workforce is not cared for?

Alex The clearest indicator that a workforce is not cared for is when I meet senior leaders that are not kind to the people, at all levels of seniority, that are immediately around them. The senior leadership have the power to create an environment where people feel cared for. If the most senior person in an organisation does not operate and function in a way that suggests that they appreciate the trauma that people are working alongside and that suggests they are not kind to those around them, that will inevitably trickle down through the workforce, like honey.

Lisa Do you think it also suggests that they are not tending to themselves and that they are also not engaged in doing that internal work that's so important?

Alex It's likely that they themselves have been socialised professionally, in organisations that function in this way. The converse, of course, is when you go into an organisation and the most senior leader, the chief executive, the director of children's services, the chair of the board, speaks kindly to the receptionist that greets them in the morning, behaves in a way that suggests that they move about the organisation, including virtually, with caution.

They make time to inquire about how people are and take steps to help people on an individual level, as well as the strategic. They have some understanding of themselves and how they present.

It is impossible when you work in an organisation with many staff to know about all of them, to know all about their lives. As leaders, we can only do what we can do with the people that are immediately around us, but when we mirror kindness and support to those we are around, others see that and respond in turn. The way in which we function influences profoundly the way in which other people function, especially as leaders. That's how we care for those that care, and create a culture where others can do the same. Leaders on every level mirror to others what it is they want from them. Leaders have followers.

Leaders are not just managers; leaders are people who have a huge influence over the way in which everyone else behaves. So how a senior leader behaves to a receptionist when they walk through the door of an organisation has an impact upon how that receptionist greets families who are experiencing crisis and trauma, later that day.

And as a consequence, when we think about things through a trauma-informed lens, we must think about doing what we can do with the people that are in front of us to function in a humane way. Now that manifests itself in this interaction that I'm describing to you now, with the people that are around themselves, but it also manifests itself on a policy level, and also manifests itself through systems such as governance, which no doubt we'll come to.

Lisa So you've been in different organisations. Think about one that you've been in that you really thought, wow, they are so good at taking care of everybody. What were the kind of key components that you saw that really made you feel like that?

Alex So it begins with this human interaction that we have with each other and the people that are in front of us on a day-to-day basis. Beyond that and into policy a very robust and very deeply interrogated well-being offer. And that's a controversial phrase because it's so often used by organisations to describe something that makes leaders feel better, because its existence suggests efforts to take care of staff, but meagre offers can be not fit for purpose. A very good example of this is counselling provided by employee assistance programmes. It is uncontroversial to suggest that those supporting families affected by trauma or crisis, actually those walking alongside and experiencing the pain of others in their relational work, should have the opportunity to explore therapeutically the impact of this upon themselves professionally and personally.

And so most organisations now, large organisations in the helping professions at least, have an employee assistance programme that provides the opportunity for therapeutic support that is confidential. And many organisations justify the support that they provide by the existence of the offer. Unfortunately, in many places, it stops there. And what leaders and managers have not interrogated is the quality of that therapeutic provision. In the worst examples, it can be four courses of online CBT where there is no human interaction whatsoever and where CBT is not the appropriate support therapeutically to provide an individual. In an inquiring organisation, it can be limitless person-centred, face-to-face therapy with a suitably qualified and experienced therapist who conducts themselves on a confidential basis and provides transformational support that enables individuals to go on to support families effectively, having received sufficient therapeutic impact themselves.

But, what we see on paper is the same thing. We see a counselling offer and we might see that in a recruitment advert and we might see leaders and managers feeling good about themselves even, because their organisation offers a counselling offer but it is night and day what is happening. So the interrogation of a well-being offer matters.

It also matters what decisions organisations make in respect of priorities; there is always only one pot of money and unfortunately this has a significant influence in respect of how organisations can provide support.

Lisa And time, because of course I have come across offers that when a person tries to take up that offer, they're not given the time and space to do so which is equally problematic in terms of that interrogation and inquiring.

Alex And after many years of leadership practice and experience, I would also argue it is not cost effective, because what happens? People leave. And when people leave, you have the on costs of recruitment, you have the on costs of training new people, and you have the inability to be able to function. You may have to pay higher agency costs.

Investing in your existing staff, providing time, space, yes, but also providing support is wholly necessary and within the gift of leaders. So I would, if one is not persuaded by the moral duty to be able to do this, think about the cost effectiveness. This applies in other ways—things like expenses policies.

It's very tempting not to put up expense rates at the level of cost of living. And what happens when we don't do that? Well, we don't support people to be able to get what they need to be able to manage their own family lives. To be able to be able to function in the workplace. And we end up in a space where the organisation just spends more money on recruitment, where there is a greater churn and where there are shortages that result in people being overstretched, so they can't provide the support they need to families.

So there is a financial investment required in respect of well-being. It needs to be considered in a very nuanced way and far beyond. For example, the consideration of counselling and into all aspects of the way in which an organisation functions from its expense policies to its annual leave policies.

Organisations, large organisations, need to have provisions in place that reflect all eventualities. How do we support staff who are affected themselves by domestic abuse? Good organisations have policies that allow for supporting people who need an advance on their salary because they fled an abusive relationship.

And, and it's not just the impact on the small number of staff who will be affected by that. This trickles down like honey; the existence of that policy in an organisation is healing to many other people who have been affected by domestic abuse, who are working with families who are affected by domestic abuse and don't get that kind of support.

And so the cost of that is close to nil, but the existence of that is profound in terms of the impact that it has on how staff feel, and how staff feel has a direct impact upon how they're able to support people who are struggling with how they feel.

Lisa Do you think we're still very stuck in this dichotomy of professional/lived experience? This idea that somehow, there are professionals, and then there are people over there with lived experience rather than understanding, as COVID highlighted very beautifully, that of course the workforce is full of people also living life, also experiencing poor health, also experiencing domestic abuse, also experiencing parenting challenges, also experiencing loss and grief and all the challenges that life brings.

Alex I think that we have come a long way in the last 20 years from where we were in respect of this issue.

And to share personally, when I first became a qualified social worker, I felt it was my professional duty to share the fact that I was a care-experienced person, given that I was working with children in care and children at risk with my managers and with some of my colleagues. I was worried about the risk of transference, subconsciously perhaps. In fact I think I was advised that, actually, by social work lecturers that it was the right thing to do to be "transparent" about that issue. I understand why, because we don't exist in a binary personal and professional self and so the impact of my experiences have the potential to impact on my practice.

Having done that for a few years, I struggled and I struggled because I found that other professionals would pathologise me. They would be very quick to say, almost half would say, immediately as they established that I was a care-experienced person, would say, why were you in care? It would be almost their first question.

And if I felt able to answer that question, I would then be pathologised. There would then be an assessment of me happening around me. I was treated then very differently sometimes with undue sympathy, perhaps, at other times in ways that were not appropriate and even discriminatory. I then started not to hide my care experience, which was a known issue by most people I've worked with, but to be much more cautious about professionally engaging that aspect of myself and asking people to be curious about why they wished to know details about my life and circumstances.

And I functioned like that for about 10 years. I think there has been a change in the last 20 years in this regard. To the extent that I'm now comfortable again drawing upon my personal experience, where it is relevant and where it helps. Some of this is about my own journey and my own confidence associated with drawing upon personal experiences to inform the professional task.

But I think we have become better at this. I do think that we need to do more to be nuanced about what we describe as lived experience. And one, just one example of that is the distinction between being influenced experts by experience who in their lives have encountered a phenomenon and those who are receiving services in the moment and giving feedback. They're both valuable, but different.

Note

The terms "lived experience," "living experience," and "experts by experience" are often used in discussions about inclusion, particularly in the fields of social work, healthcare, and community services. Each term highlights different aspects of personal expertise based on direct involvement and insights. Here's a breakdown:

1. **Lived Experience**
   - **Definition**: Refers to personal knowledge about the world gained through direct, firsthand involvement in everyday events.
   - **Context**: Often used to describe individuals who have firsthand experience with specific issues, such as mental health conditions, addiction, homelessness, or disability.
   - **Focus**: Emphasises the historical and ongoing impact of these experiences on the individual's life and perspective.
2. **Living Experience**
   - **Definition**: Similar to lived experience, but emphasises the current and ongoing nature of the experience.
   - **Context**: Used to highlight that the individual is actively and presently dealing with or navigating a particular situation.
   - **Focus**: Stresses the continuous and evolving nature of the experience, rather than it being solely in the past.
3. **Experts by Experience**
   - **Definition**: Individuals who use their lived or living experiences to provide insights, advice, or guidance in professional or advocacy settings.
   - **Context**: Often engaged in roles that involve consultation, training, policy-making, or peer support based on their experiential knowledge.
   - **Focus**: Recognises these individuals as valuable contributors who offer practical wisdom and insights that can improve services, policies, and practices.

> **Key Differences**
>
> - **Temporal Aspect**: "Lived experience" can encompass past and present, while "living experience" specifically underscores the ongoing nature of the experience.
> - **Role and Application**: "Experts by experience" highlights a functional role where individuals actively contribute their insights to shape and improve systems and practices.
>
> Using these terms accurately helps ensure that personal narratives are respected and appropriately integrated into broader conversations and decision-making processes. Each term brings a unique perspective that is essential for comprehensive, empathetic, and effective engagement in various fields.

          There's great value in someone, sometime later, feeling able to draw upon what their experience means for themselves and potentially the professional task, either theirs or others. And feedback from those who are experiencing something in the moment also offers immediate value. And for me, they're very different. And I still think we talk about lived experiences as if it's one homogenous thing.

Lisa   Can you imagine on your social work training being asked to disclose whether you were poverty experienced or whether your parents had divorced or whether you had had difficulties at school or a whole other range of experience?

          I do think that the care experience is particularly an area that has been focused upon differently because of the stigmatisation (and sometimes exploited) and therefore appears to raise the most concern for people from a kind of safeguarding perspective. Alternatively, to you, I mentioned it twice, got such bad responses that I didn't talk about it really again for years in professional settings. That's how I handled it until I became self-employed in 2010.

So finally, we've talked about leadership. Do you think there is an unnecessary distinction between leadership and management?

This book really focuses on leadership, but of course within that, there are lots of people who are going to be managers. In your experience, and from the work that you're currently looking at, what would you say are the key differences between leadership and management?

Alex The binary that's often presented to us is that a manager is somebody who instructs, somebody who requires, somebody who looks at data and spreadsheets, somebody who manages. A leader is somebody who has followers, somebody who is visionary, somebody who is inspirational. The difficulty for organisations is that both of those things are required. The encouragement towards leadership in the absence of the management task would leave organisations without governance and therefore put staff and the people that they serve at risk. It would leave organisations without line managers and therefore have no annual leave authorised or expenses claims signed off.

It is my view that you can be both, that organisations need both functions and that we make a mistake when we describe an individual as either a manager or a leader. I have had a successful career looking at spreadsheets, managing budgets, giving instruction, whilst also, I believe, leading services, developing people, creating and leading on vision. But I learnt early on, as they say, that culture trumps strategy every time.

So I am uncomfortable with the binary debate that exists that suggests that people are either managers or leaders, that individuals have to choose one or the other or be better at one or the other. My view is that organisations need both and that it is unhelpful for us to think on an individual level that we can only be one or the other.

Lisa That's so interesting because I often find myself saying that where we are seeking to create a culture change, we need leaders, not managers. So I'm fascinated by this idea that people who have got very clear management-operational ways of doing are also able to focus on culture change. Leadership often requires sticking your head above the parapet, going against the grain, doing things differently. Different skills are required, so I am very happy to hear that you feel that one person can do all of that, all of that in one.

Alex I also feel that seniority is irrelevant. I'll give you one of the most profound examples of leadership that I can think of. And it was a woman who'd worked in an organisation for 20 years, who welcomed children and families to her place of work every day.

And those children and families were in a difficult place as a result of them needing to engage with that service; they were experiencing crisis, they had experienced trauma, they were in a very difficult situation. And unbeknown to anybody for about 15 years she made sure that every child that played with a colouring pencil had a sharp one to play with by sharpening each of them.

She personally cleaned the space if she didn't feel it was clean enough and over time, the social workers, the health visitors, the psychologists, the managers, the doctors, the other people who came to this place started treating it equally with respect. She did this very quietly for 5, 10, 15 years, making sure that everything was perfect in that place.

She was one of the greatest leaders that I worked with and she was paid just above minimum wage. Leadership is about seeing something that needs to happen and sometimes quietly, sometimes loudly enacting a vision, sometimes an unpopular one, sometimes when there's no money and as a consequence of that, other people start following. That's what leadership is. That's all it is. It isn't complicated. It doesn't need to be. It doesn't need a strategy. It doesn't need a conference. It is about doing ourselves something that we would want others to do. It is eminently possible to do that alongside being a manager.

What we should be saying is we need leadership. We do need "the idea," we need the constructs, we need those behaviours to exist. But organisations do still need people to write budgets, to have governance, to sign off annual leave, to sign expenses! Those managers can also be leaders and, day in, day out, are doing a great job for the people that they support.

Lisa Well, I'm very much of the view that leadership is not a job title. The ability to operate from a place of leadership *and* be a manager is going to be what we're all hoping organisations who work with people requiring services are full of.

> **Reflection**
>
> Overall, this conversation has emphasised the interconnectedness of leadership behaviour, systemic support, and the integration of personal experiences in creating a supportive and effective organisational culture. There is a real need, in caring for the people that care, for a thoughtful, comprehensive approach to employee well-being that goes beyond surface-level solutions to address the deeper needs and challenges faced by all members of the community.

> **Discussion Points**
>
> 1. **Leadership Influence**
>   - Leaders set the tone for the organisation with their behaviour. What tone are you setting?
>   - How do your interactions integrate kindness and influence the overall organisational culture?
> 2. **Human Interaction and Policy**
>   - Daily human interactions are crucial, but policies and systems also play a significant role. What do your policies reflect about your organisation?
>   - How robust and well-interrogated is your well-being offer, especially for those dealing with trauma?
> 3. **Counselling and Support**
>   - Is your Employee Assistance Program of high quality?
>   - Does the counselling offer move beyond the superficial to provide meaningful, person-centred therapy?

4. **Financial and Time Investment**
   - In what ways does your orgaisation invest in staff well-being?
   - Providing time, space, and support for employees is crucial to prevent burnout and turnover. Is this understood by your organisation?
5. **Comprehensive Policies**
   - How comprehensive and flexible are policies that support staff reflecting various life situations, such as dealing with domestic abuse?
   - How are staff made aware of such policies?
6. **Integration of Lived Experience**
   - In what ways is it understood that practitioners often have lived experiences that impact their practice?
   - How are these experiences acknowledged and integrated into professional roles without pathologising individuals?
7. **Integrating Leadership and Management**
   - How do I balance operational responsibility with the vision and influence required for effective leadership?
   - In what ways might I unknowingly reinforce the unhelpful binary between "leader" and "manager" in my own practice or expectations of others?
8. **Everyday Acts of Leadership**
   - Who are the "quiet leaders" in my organisation, and how might I better recognise and value their contribution?
   - How can I cultivate a culture where leadership is recognised in all roles, regardless of title or pay grade?

PART TWO
Belonging

6
Introduction to Part Two

I wouldn't have been able to write about how we care for each other without a section on belonging. Belonging is the focus of my research and the subject of my last book, *Weaving a Web of Belonging*. We live and work in a world shaped by systems of exclusion and inequality and unbelonging. Whether we are conscious of this or not, these systems show up in our language, our policies, our classrooms, our clinics, our team meetings, and our moments of silence. This section of the book asks you to pause, reflect, and choose again and to begin to notice what needs to be different in your setting, service, or system to take active steps toward repair, justice, and healing.

Moving beyond and intersecting with, thinking about, belonging, there is a whole body of work exploring "mattering" and the implications of not mattering. If you've ever walked into a room and felt invisible, or been in a conversation where your presence didn't seem to register, you've brushed against what it means not to matter. And if you've ever felt completely accepted, safe to be yourself, and recognised as a meaningful part of something bigger, you've felt the power of belonging. These are not sentimental concepts. They are foundational to human well-being.

Belonging and mattering are core human psychological needs, as vital as food, water, or shelter. When people feel like they don't belong, when they believe they don't matter, their nervous systems stay on high alert. This has profound implications for emotional regulation, learning, behaviour, and physical health. As Flett, Heisel, and Zuroff note: "Mattering is a vital construct and a key psychological resource that is central to the human condition; indeed, the individual person who lives his or her life devoid of a sense of mattering to others will lack the basic sense of personal significance, human connectedness, and social acceptance required to thrive and flourish" (Flett, 2021). From a mental health perspective, mattering sits at the heart of many common struggles. People who consistently receive the message that they do not matter, whether through direct harm, microaggressions, lack of voice, or institutional neglect, often internalise these experiences. Over time, they may begin to believe that they are a problem to be managed, rather than a person with gifts and insight to offer. This can lead to long-term psychological effects including low self-worth, increased anxiety, depressive symptoms, and, in some cases, self-harm or suicidal ideation.

In trauma-informed work, this understanding reshapes our approach. When people feel like they are just one of many, reduced to a label or a task, they are more likely to disengage. But when they feel like they are seen and significant, even in small ways, they begin to feel safe and cared for.

It's important to understand that mattering is both emotional and structural. A person may feel emotionally supported by someone but still experience systemic devaluation through racist policies, inaccessible services, or homophobic environments. We therefore have to work across all domains and levels, creating compassionate interactions while also changing the systems that routinely tell people they don't count.

This includes racial and cultural identity, gender diversity, neurodivergence, disability, socioeconomic status, and other intersecting identities. Representation must also be active, not just symbolic, through co-creation of programmes, resources, and environments. True equity means building structures where diverse voices are not only welcomed but woven into the fabric of our work.

Introduction to Part Two

This section takes you on that journey. Millie talks about her powerful anti-racist strategic action planning work in Brighton and Hove, while Hira focuses on Islamophobia and generously provides many solutions to a better understanding of the impact of Islamophobia and the importance of allyship. Jane shares about her role in decolonising practice in her setting while Karen explores intergenerational and ancestral trauma.

Belonging is a human motivational need and we will find a way to belong and if we can't, the consequences will be felt by all.

Reference

Flett, G. L. (2021). An introduction, review, and conceptual analysis of mattering as an essential construct and an essential way of life. *Journal of Psychoeducational Assessment*, 40(1), 3–36.

7

A Conversation With Millie Kerr

The Implications and Need of Anti-Racist Strategic Action Planning

Millie begins this section on belonging, opening up how we might consider the implications and need of anti-racist strategic action planning. Millie sets out a plan for how this might be developed in other settings, drawing from what has worked well in her Local Authority.

Lisa Millie, so tell me a little bit about your work.

Millie I am a registered social worker with over 30 years' experience as a practitioner and as a manager. Much of this period has been spent working with many diverse and Black and Global Majority people and communities.

I have always been interested in working with the most marginalised and sometimes hidden groups or communities. My career thus far has involved working as a social work practitioner in children's safeguarding, with asylum seekers and refugee's children and young people, child trafficking and HIV and FGM/C services, within local authority and voluntary sector settings, in addition to holding management and senior management roles over the past 20 years. Prior to qualifying as a social worker, I have also spent a fair amount of time within youth and community work, residential work within children disability services, as well as mental health.

At a time when HIV services were limited for women and children living with and impacted by HIV, I supported the development of Black women's groups as part of service development for an organisation called Blackliners, which provided support to Black communities, which sadly no longer exists.

I presently am employed as the strategic anti-racist lead within Brighton & Hove City Council, a post I was promoted into, in August 2023, with the remit of continuing to develop strategic action plans that will widen the reach of anti-racist practice within children's services and with multi-agency partners. To support learning and culture change within the workforce, to enable better and improved support and services, to Black and Global Majority children's families and communities.

We need to move toward being more explicit and put more action behind DEI, or diversity, equality, and inclusion strategies, which have been in danger for some time, of just becoming a tick box exercise with no real substance for supporting a real appetite for change, in giving Black and Global Majority people a real seat at the table. So, I feel that the work I am doing, around developing anti-racist practice within my present role and within my growing training and consultancy business, feels like a calling that I must answer and where I have been given the autonomy and opportunity to cultivate real action and culture change. I am under no illusion however that this will be a lifelong goal, as we are not going to fix racism and inequity in my lifetime.

The work I do can be stressful, emotive, isolating, and can take a lot from me, so I need to ensure I care for myself. In doing so I do have support internally within my working environment and outside of my working environment.

The work I've been doing within the local authority and at a national level has encompassed looking at workforce development, organisation culture change, and enhancing practice.

Lisa What does that look like?

Millie In terms of anti-racist strategic action planning, the aim is to enable local authority children's services in Brighton to develop their anti-racist practice starting with the workforce. Looking at privilege and how we support the recruitment, development, and retention of Black and Global Majority staff members. For example, a rough action plan can consider, "How do you support your staff members and their learning?" "How do you support your children and families or Adults?" "How do you listen to the voices of children, families, and communities?" In considering these three questions how are you enabling what may predominantly be a white workforce to learn about biases, stereotypes, in addition to considering how to provide better support and opportunities to Black staff members. The other two questions try to get the workforce to look at how they can engage better in terms of their direct work, understanding different cultural norms, as well as considering what may need to be adapted or changed, in terms of the Eurocentric lens used to view others and the systems and processes we use. Lastly, how do we really consider engagement with communities, and listening and actioning change from staff and service user feedback and audits?

On a practical and strategic level, this may encompass delivering training on issues such as Adultification and safeguarding, stereotypes and working with Black dads, microaggressions, white privilege, and the impact of racial trauma on Black children and families. Supporting services to have uncomfortable conversations about race, within safe/brave spaces (team meetings, group supervisions). Supporting the recruitment, development, retention, and progression of Black and Global Majority staff members. By engaging in strategic development groups within my local authority, via the Workforce Race Equality Standard (WRES). In addition to supporting the development of support groups for staff members with lived experiences of racism and discrimination, to include the intersectional considerations of supporting our international social workers.

From a national perspective, delivering anti-racist training, keynote presentations, and workshops to different local authorities, the charity/voluntary sector and national conferences such as Community Care Live, Research in Practice, and BASW World Social Work Day workshops have proved to be influential in spreading the benefits of developing anti-racist practice within the workforce. Which in term aids improvements in how we engage, support, and build trust with Black and Global Majority communities and other marginalised groups.

Lisa So that's a huge amount of experience to draw upon. I have two questions because this book is very much focused on how we support our workforce. I've just been in a meeting where one of the things that people highlighted was that they think that we're still not getting where we need to in terms of taking care of our staff.

You talked about what this work takes from you and you are incredibly aware of what this work takes from those that work within your local authority. Do you want to talk a little bit about what you've seen and what you're working on to support those working in the local authority?

Millie A lot of what I'm trying to do is to impact ongoing learning around anti-racist practice and thinking to embed culture change. By supporting uncomfortable conversations about race, stereotypes, biases, assumptions, and labels, we may unwittingly or wittingly ascribe to people who may look different from the perceived white norm of our workforce or society. We have made an impact on shifting thinking and some practice within children's services, but there is still a long way to go, particularly as regards how we develop equity and better inclusion right through to senior leadership positions within organisations.

However, in considering some of the questions posed previously, which can be used as the beginning of developing anti-racist strategies and action plans, I will talk about what we have done to enhance anti-racist practice within the workforce under "Staff Support."

When considering staff support and why the local authority wanted to develop a fair and inclusive and anti-racist action plan, there first needed to be recognition that there was inequity around Black and Global Majority staff members going through capabilities and performance. In addition to children, families, and audits citing that our communities viewed engagement with services as racist. With the organisation wanting to do something to change this view by taking some concrete action toward change. This also meant recognising that staff members from Black, Asian, and Global Majority backgrounds, as well as our children and families, had lived experiences of racism and discrimination and how were we going to listen and learn from uncomfortable truths and conversations to aid staff and service improvement?

We held engagement, listening events, and surveys with staff members, incorporating our BME Forums views, along with what changes Black staff members wanted to see to feel heard. A decision was taken to not just have a fair and inclusive action plan council wide and anti-racist action plan for children's services, but to also recruit an anti-racist lead and strategic anti-racist business improvement, to impact operational and strategic change within the workforce. White senior leaders/staff read and worked through *Me and My White Supremacy*, Layla Saad,[1] looking at white privilege, before rolling it out to all team managers and children's services teams within the service. With Black and Global Majority staff members having separate reading groups, before going back to their teams to continue discussions about learning and support. Anti-racist discussion groups were developed and are ongoing monthly for all staff in children's services to attend to have conversations about race, racism, links to social work practice, and support and direct work to BGM children and families.

In recognising that Black and Global Majority staff members experience racism and discrimination within the organisation, as well as from the families and communities we serve, we also set up monthly support groups for staff to come together for peer support, networking, development, as well as celebrations (bring and share lunch, Black history month, social events etc.). Regular opportunities to feed up to senior leaders are also in place for staff to feed up any issues of concern, which has impacted some change and improvements to staff support. The impact of racial trauma on BGM staff members has also been recognised, with agreement to secure regular emotional support from a Black psychotherapist, for a period for BGM staff members with lived experience of racism and discrimination.

We also have an "Anti-racist project board" made up of senior leaders and BGM social workers, who meet monthly to monitor and review progress of our anti-racist action plan.

In addition, we have been undertaking blind/anonymous shortlisting of candidates for social work roles, whereby we have no details about an applicant's name or ethnicity, other than a HR reference number, until we have completed shortlisted candidates. Also ensuring that we have diversity, and a staff member from a BGM background on our interview panels, wherever possible. To engender the potential for the development and progression of BGM staff members, the development of a "Diverse leaders programme," which has begun to see BGM staff members promoted into more senior social work/managerial positions.

The aforementioned is just a few examples of how we consider "staff support" and ongoing learning around anti-racist practice. From my perspective, it's about how we can really listen to what staff and communities are saying, with a willingness to learn and change and in Brighton children's services, we are at least on that trajectory.

From my perspective, people can listen, take note of audits, data, and read reports/research that talk about underrepresentation, or overrepresentation of certain groups, that may talk about racism, racial trauma inequity in employment, service delivery, etc., but are they actually hearing? To hear and take note means there must

A Conversation With Millie Kerr

be a willingness and a wish to take action, impact culture change, for real inclusion and a sense of belonging to be realised.

Lisa What is the impact upon people who continuously talk about and share what's going on for them as they fill out surveys, complete forms, have meetings, and yet are still not heard, demonstrated through there being tokenistic or no action? I've seen this with research, I've seen this with children and adults with care experience across many years. While I think there have been improvements in the ethics of how we gather knowledge from those with lived experiences, we're still on a journey. Not being heard has an impact, doesn't it?

Millie Absolutely, and my gosh does not being heard cause fatigue! As well as a reluctance to get involved in diversity and inclusion initiatives, anger, or a wish to be silent, due to the sense that we just go round in circles, regurgitating the same questions and surveys with no real change, other than what can feel like another annual, DEI tick box exercise. If I just focus on where I am now, there has been some listening and hearing, which has translated into action within children's services.

All of the work we have been doing with our Black, Global Majority and international social workers has been important to provide them with a sense of belonging and that they are being heard, even if we are unable fix everything needed to end discrimination and racism. This support has been instrumental in encouraging staff retention. The impact of racial trauma, caused by day-to-day experiences of racism and oppression, has been recognised within children's services. Particularly when this may not just manifest within the working environment but may also be experienced when undertaking their social work role and duties with families and the communities we serve, and as employees of the council. So Black and Global Majority support groups have been important, as a safe space where staff can feel heard, listened to, supported, and understood without judgement.

We also provide additional emotional support to staff via a Black psychotherapist; that provides staff members to consider the impact of racial trauma in their work. Which may not continue indefinitely but was another example of senior leaders within the authority, listening to the needs of its BGM workforce, which I have found to be quite rare in many local authorities.

In terms of the wider council, Brighton remains on a journey toward becoming an anti-racist local authority and toward developing our council-wide anti-racist strategy into all areas of the council. Also considering protected characteristics through an intersectional lens.

Lisa What was it about considering racial trauma that was problematic, do you think? I think when we talk about trauma-informed practice, people miss and are not sure or maybe don't understand the element of trauma-informed work that focuses on racial trauma.

Millie When we talk about trauma-informed practice, people do not always recognise or understand the impact racism can have on individuals' mental health and well-being. Neither the accumulative impact that may start from age three in nursery, being told your skin colour "looks like poo." The nursery is not comfortable in dealing with that or just say, "oh they're only babies, they don't understand what they are saying." That child then goes to primary school and racist bullying continues and is now saying, "I don't like my hair, I want my hair cut off." Then goes home to his parents and says, "oh, I wish I was white," as they can already see the inequity and experience the difference in treatment due to their race. This continues through to secondary school and continues to not be dealt with appropriately. There may be unaddressed or unrecognised issues around neurodiversity which are also not considered. Then the "behaviour" of Black children and adults becomes a concern and the main focus, not the cause, and Black children and adults can then be viewed through a stereotypical lens of being a problem. So, children may get angry out of frustration and lack of support, become silent, due to thinking there's no point in speaking up, no one is listening, or, in the work environment, will just leave their job to find another. No one is listening to the emotional impact, the impact on mental health, then not feeling as if you belong and dismissing harms caused to Black children through verbal and emotional abuse.

I've looked at a piece of research that came out of Georgia, and racial trauma can be defined as, "The negative effects of racial discrimination and the unfair or prejudicial treatment of individuals on the basis of race."[2] The accumulative impact of racial abuse in all its forms caused trauma, and, to ensure Black and Global Majority staff are appropriately supported, as well as the children, families, and communities we serve, this needs to be properly understood. To this aim, that is why we have not just put in place emotional support for our staff members as indicated previously. There is now a willingness to learn more about how racial trauma impacts our children, families, and communities, so we will also be delivering a series of racial trauma training sessions for social workers in children's services. To develop all staff's understanding of this type of trauma and its impact on children and adults.

There can be an expectation that people should just assimilate into "how we do things here," but what can we learn, by looking outside of Eurocentric values, theories, and norms, about others' experiences, their lived experiences of oppression to enable individuals? To enable organisations to provide better support, looking through a racial trauma, not just a trauma-informed lens. The work I do around anti-racist practice is by no means perfect, but it has begun to widen the lens of individuals' views and perceptions of people who look different to the perceived predominantly white workforce and through the lens of biases and stereotypes. Therefore, personally, I am pleased that we are on the journey to being open to listening and learning about racial trauma, so that we can support our BGM staff and communities better.

The recent census from 2021 shows the biggest growth community in Brighton, since the last census, was "mixed and multiple mixed ethnic groups, rising from 3.8% in 2011 to 4.8% of the population in 2021."[3] With a similar figure for Asian and Asian British communities within the city. This data has also formed part of our thinking in developing social work practice within children's services, around working with and enhancing children and young people's cultural identity, religion, and sense of belonging in their direct work. Also starting from the premise that these children and families will have lived experience of racism, as immigrants to the UK, asylum seekers, refugees, or due to the colour of their race or religion. Creating safe spaces within our work and teams to have uncomfortable conversations, to develop a better understanding about racial trauma, particularly within a predominantly white workforce. These conversations assist in building the confidence of our workforce to challenge racism, having difficult conversations, and increasing trusting relationships and change, when working with all our Global Majority communities.

We will not make real progress within our society, when we hear continuous racist ideology that traumatises Black, Asian, and marginalised communities. Racist ideology and comments from government leaders, about different religions, cultures, and people from Black, Caribbean, African, Chinese backgrounds, etc., can still be publicly made. Where whiteness is held up and viewed as superior and whiteness is viewed as the dominant race and others who may look different are viewed through an inferior lens. This perception in itself can compound people's experiences of racial trauma and sense of belonging.

Everything around us, particularly at this point and time in our history, treats difference as inferior. There have been some comments made, even by our politicians, which impact racial trauma in our wider society that even if you are born in the UK, you are still othered. When people have been "asked" to come and help rebuild Britain after the Second World War you are still othered and experience the trauma from racist comments, such as "alien cultures" and "bringing in their medieval ways" by mainstream politicians. We need to do better and I know that this will take a lifetime.

Lisa I heard those comments too and what I heard was fascism.

Let me take you back to racial trauma because the question I asked you—and I appreciate you might not feel comfortable answering this because you're employed by the local authority—but what I'm interested in is why there's a discomfort with thinking about racial trauma in the context that you've just described, what is it that you think is the resistance to that?

Millie   I suppose it's not been complete resistance, it has been more about how to frame the support, as it has been support provided in a more group supervision context than considering it as clinical supervision, around supporting racial trauma within the work environment. There was a commitment to providing this support to BGM social workers within children's services, as I have mentioned previously. The concern was more around clarity of what could and couldn't be provided for staff during the allotted reflective group time. With staff members needing to access additional support if needed, via the council's counselling support or via their GP. As previously stated, and to aid the wider workforce understanding of racial trauma and its impact, we will be delivering training to our social workers within children's services.

When I am talking to staff and trying to get them to look through an anti-racist and racial trauma lens, I often ask about how they feel about talking about race or the topic I may have raised about race or discrimination, to get them to think more deeply about where the feelings or views come from. This is a starting point for me to get staff uncomfortable with the feelings that they may not think about and that may be being experienced by the Black colleagues or children, families, or communities they are working with. This in turn gets people thinking about the questions they may ask BGM communities that they may just expect an answer to without thinking through their experiences, why they may mistrust social workers. Why do you not want to answer the question or do not want to engage, where I may then say, Black communities are not difficult to engage; it's about "how" you try to engage people that is the key. The objective being to get individuals, managers, and senior leaders to look beyond presenting behaviours to look at cause and the why, which is being trauma informed in their practice. Without allowing labels, stereotypes, bias, and assumptions to tarnish their thinking and to remain open to different perspectives and hypothesis, which may be impacted by individuals' lived experiences. White staff have not been used to looking at culture or race through a white lens, so it has been beneficial to enable this process to happen, to bring clarity to the racial trauma experienced by people due to their race, religion, or culture and how they can be treated differently as a result.

We're getting people to look at the trauma, caused through language, in terms of how we speak and write about people, in terms of the decisions we make etc. Enabling white staff in particular to see that racism and racial trauma can be experienced by people on an individual level and on a macro bigger level. If I use the example witnessing the murder of George Floyd, that impacted and traumatised many people, but particularly me and many other Black people who began to feel unsafe as if our lives didn't matter. Similar community impacts of racial trauma were also experienced by Black communities, Muslim communities, and by asylum seekers and refugees, during the far-right violence of the summer of 2024. Feeling unsafe, feeling like you cannot leave your home, feeling that you cannot allow your children to leave or go far from home. Not having to give your Black son/child "the talk," which many Black Caribbean families do, in explaining to their children how to behave if they are stopped and searched by the police, because they want them to come home safely. These are all examples of the impact of racial trauma and examples of white privilege. In that many white families may not have to live with the same fear, due to the colour of their skin. A trauma and racially trauma-informed organisation would consider these fears and allow their Black staff members to work from home, offer buddies to travel with them on public transport, or have managers offer to pick up and drive Black staff to work if needed, as was the case in supporting our Black colleagues in Brighton children's services.

It may seem like a long-winded answer to your question, but it has given me the opportunity to think about what allyship or solidarity looks like when I sometimes feel as if it can be performative within local authorities and organisations. As these examples show, it's important to have some insight into understanding the impact of trauma on our BGM staff members and communities in terms of what interventions can look like to show your support, willingness to learn, look through other's eyes even if you never experience racism yourself, there needs to be the ability to empathise, so support inclusion and belonging.

Lisa We've talked a lot about being heard, haven't we, and what happens to us when we're not heard and when we're not seen and heard.

Millie I think these are the four important things that need to happen from my perspective. As well as being *listened* to and *hearing* lived experiences of trauma, it is important to always be *curious* and understanding about the impact and make *time* to consider appropriate support and action that needs to be taken.

Embedding anti-racist practice into organisations is not easy; it's uncomfortable and there may be some resistance in getting people to think about what they don't have to think about, particularly if you're white. However, creating safe or brave spaces to have uncomfortable conversations, talk about race and how you can better engage communities and build trust, can only be a good thing. Race is a white construct; let's break it down, accept each other's differences, cultures, religions, customs, and norms, so that there will come a time in history, where we will all be considered as part of the "human race."

Lisa There is a lot of training that doesn't talk about historical trauma, racial trauma, colonisation impact, the legacy of slavery, intergenerational trauma, all of those things and it deeply concerns me. It deeply concerns me when people don't want to talk about these things but what I've noticed, when I do talk about those areas, is that the discomfort in the room is palpable.

I think because people from all sorts of backgrounds may be thinking about that impact for the first time. And if we're thinking about how we also take care of the people we're working with, there is a duty upon us to also go very gently about how impacted they may well have been.

Millie This is very true, and we are in the position we are in now within society, with much division, inequity, othering discrimination, and racism, because of colonialism, power, capitalism, intergenerational historical trauma, racial trauma, and attempts to erase parts of Black history. When I am delivering external training now to different organisations, I am much more explicit in getting people to understand racism beyond just looking through a DEI lens, by getting people to consider who can often be deemed superior or inferior within our society.

Racism definition – the Oxford Dictionary defines *racism* as: Prejudice, discrimination, or antagonism directed against someone of a different race based on the belief that one's own race is superior.

When we talk about discomfort and having uncomfortable conversations, white staff members may not find it comfortable, but neither will Black staff members, who will often have lived experience of racism, within the work environment and within the communities we serve.

We can no longer tread or go quietly when discussing the oppression of people due to the colour of their skin, ethnic group, or due to their religious beliefs.

When we're thinking about anti-racist practice and racial trauma, you have to start the learning by looking at yourself, particularly if you are white. Reflecting on where stereotypes, biases, and beliefs come from and educating oneself about differences as well as unlearning beliefs about people and cultures you may have grown up with, in addition to distorted and racist views that can be portrayed by the media and social media. We can be good at talking about trauma-informed practice, and racial trauma, but do we really understand it or really take the time to think about what this means in practice and when working with Black communities?

Whiteness is perceived to be the norm in our society, but there is another worldview which I have adopted and find empowering, even though I recognise I may still be a minority in many settings. That is why I use the term *Black and Global Majority*.

According to Wikipedia, the definition of *Global Majority* is "a collective term for people of African, Asian, Indigenous, Latin American, or mixed-heritage backgrounds, who constitute approximately 85% of the global population." There is a video developed by Rosemary Campbell-Stephens MBE that is worth watching.[4]

Does this not give an insight into how powerful white supremacy, colonialism, and empire was? How countries led by white kings, queens, and leaders dominated huge parts of the world, enslaved people who were viewed as inferior, whilst reaping the riches and minerals of their lands for their own, in the name of exploration, trade, and ownership. By the mere fact that our royal family and King Charles III remains head of the Commonwealth, that in itself speaks to the history of the 52 countries that were once colonised by Britain, under the British empire, before many gained their independence. A big part of becoming anti-racist in one's practice is to learn about all of one's history, the good and the bad.

It is also not enough to say you are "not racist"; you must be "anti-racist," in challenging injustice and racism wherever you may see it or hear it and not being a bystander. No matter how small your action toward change might be. You must also try to be an ally and stand in solidarity with your Black and Global Majority colleagues, peers, family, and the communities you serve to impact lasting change. Not just for a moment in time, at the injustice of the murder of George Floyd or against the far-right violence of the summer of 2024, but all of the time, so that we can begin to eradicate hate, inequity, and injustice one issue and with one individual at a time.

Lisa We've mentioned that one of the things that you do that you would highlight as a good practice for your workforce is that you've been providing a psychotherapist. What else have you been doing that would highlight good practice for the workforce?

Millie. We have created safe spaces, which was weekly initially online, for all staff and particularly our white staff members to join and engage in an anti-racist discussion. These drop-in sessions set up to have uncomfortable and brave conversations are now held monthly, in person to engender richer discussions and reflections. At the different office bases within the children service's directorate, to ensure we are including as many staff members as possible. These anti-racist drop-ins are not just for social work staff; senior leaders and business support staff also attend periodically.

The discussions have ranged from working with Black dads, how to support the identity needs of missed heritage children and young people, adultification bias, why are there no Black women in our domestic violence services, etc.

We've also been doing a lot of work around adultification bias and safeguarding (Davis, 2022). Recently developing joint training with our adolescent, youth justice service, and our police. Highlighting the impact of adultification and racial trauma, stop and search on our young people. This has also supported the building of relationships and understanding across our multi-agency partnerships.

We also have training/workshops on topics such as working with Black dads, because there are stereotypes of Black dads; they're aggressive, they are gangsters, drug dealers. Getting social workers and the wider workforce to think about the language they're using, to describe parents and children, in a more trauma-informed way, when there can be a tendency to focus on assessing children's needs and safeguarding concerns, through the mother/primary carer lens. This has now been culminating in having regular monthly online sessions looking at how social work staff work better with all dads within social work assessments. Language and how we use it, particularly within reports and assessments, is important.

Our senior leaders have reflective reading groups monthly, to reflect on race and racism to enhance their continued learning around anti-racist practice. Moving on from reading *Me and My White Supremacy* (2022) to books such as *The Good Ally* (Reid, 2021). Using this and other books to make links with their practice and continued service improvement ideas. In addition, our social work teams have regular anti-racist group supervisions, where children and families may be discussed in a reflective group, to consider improved engagement, challenges, or seek support around understanding cultural differences or in undertaking direct work with Black, Asian, and Global Majority children and families.

I also ensure we are considering and preparing for DEI initiatives that may be coming up in the calendar year annually, such as Race Equality Week (REW), International Women's Day, and Black History Month. Organising lunch and learn sessions, for REW, for example, for the workforce, including senior leaders, covering issues such as microaggressions and intersectionality more recently and their impact on Black and Global Majority staff members within the organisation. Encouraging all in attendance to always consider what action they are going to take at the end of the sessions, to enhance inclusion and their anti-racist practice, within their service or as part of their own individual learning.

Our Black staff members will also organise social events and bring and share events, which enhances their sense of feeling valued and a sense of belonging within the work environment. We have a long way to go, but we are on the journey toward organisational culture change, with the support of our senior leaders and allies.

Lisa   Thank you so much. There is so much there to support people who may be at the beginning of this journey or want to add movement to the journey they're already on.

Reflection

Millie provides so many ways that an organisation can care for Black staff members, cultivating belonging and mattering, whether that's through a book club, providing a psychotherapist, or through training, workshops, and safe spaces. What Millie highlights so well is that the work is intentional. It doesn't just happen.

Discussion Points

- **Embedding Anti-Racist Practice Strategically**
  - How is my organisation moving beyond performative equality, diversity, and inclusion (EDI) statements to implement anti-racist strategies with measurable impact?
  - In what ways does our action planning reflect the lived experiences of Black and Global Majority staff and communities?
- **Listening, Hearing, and Acting**
  - How do I ensure that listening to staff and communities leads to meaningful change, rather than contributing to fatigue and disillusionment?
  - What mechanisms exist in my workplace to gather feedback—and are they matched by structures that ensure follow-through and accountability?
- **Understanding and Responding to Racial Trauma**
  - Do I fully understand the concept of racial trauma, and how is it addressed (or overlooked) in my organisation's trauma-informed approach?
  - How might our current policies and practices unintentionally ignore or minimise the emotional impact of racism on staff, children, and families?

- **Building Cultures of Belonging and Equity**
  - What am I doing in my role to ensure Black and Global Majority staff feel a genuine sense of belonging, safety, and opportunity?
  - How do we recognise and amplify leadership and expertise from those with lived experience of racism and oppression across all levels of the organisation?
- **Racial Trauma and the Role of Social Work**
  - How confident am I in recognising and responding to racial trauma in my work with children, families, and colleagues?
  - In what ways does my current social work practice acknowledge or overlook the impact of structural and intergenerational racism?
- **Beyond Diversity: Towards Genuine Allyship and Anti-Racism**
  - Am I showing up as a true ally, or am I participating in performative gestures without lasting impact?
  - What practical actions have I taken (or could take) to challenge racism and demonstrate anti-racist values in my everyday role?
- **Identity, Belonging, and Cultural Understanding**
  - How am I supporting the cultural identity, religion, and belonging of mixed heritage, refugee, asylum-seeking, or immigrant children and families?
  - How do I challenge assumptions or stereotypes in myself or others when engaging with children and families from diverse backgrounds?
- **Creating Brave Spaces and Shifting Organisational Culture**
  - What opportunities exist within my team or organisation to have honest, reflective, and challenging conversations about race and racism—and do I engage in them?
  - How is my organisation actively creating an environment where discomfort can lead to growth, particularly for white staff learning about anti-racism?

Notes

1 https://laylafsaad.com/meandwhitesupremacy.
2 Coping with Racial Trauma | The Department of Psychology. https://psychology.uga.edu/coping-racial-trauma.
3 https://www.ons.gov.uk/visualisations/censusareachanges/E06000043/.
4 Global Majority. https://www.youtube.com/watch?v=D_8bnTiUGI0.

References

Davis, J. (2022). *Adultification Bias within Child Protection and Safeguarding*. HMI Probation.
Reid, N. (2021). *The Good Ally*. Harper Collins Publishers.

8
A Conversation With Hira Ali

Recognising and Addressing Islamophobia

Throughout writing this book, the social and political context of the time we are living has intensified. In the summer of 2024, the UK experienced racial violence in ways that felt very different to what we had seen before. The anti-Muslim and Islamophobic rhetoric found a space to shout its abuse from and this time, it wasn't just about the "far right."

The inauguration of Donald Trump as president of the US in January 2025 brought the cancellation of USAID,[1] a declaration that Gaza should be owned by the US, and that Palestinians should simply leave their homeland with no right to return.[2] He has signed three executive orders (EOs) seeking to end diversity, equity, and inclusion (DEI) programmes in the public and private sectors, declaring DEI programmes "illegal and immoral."

Europe has six countries currently with hard right parties in government.[3] The impact of what some might call a rise in fascism will be felt by the workforce. Some of the workforce will feel it more sharply than others and how it is supported, understood, and heard will make the greatest difference.

Lisa   You've written several bodies of work that focus on supporting Muslim women, allyship, and noticing Islamophobia. How did you come to do that work?

Hira   When I moved to the UK about eight and a half years ago, I'll admit that I initially resisted being seen as the poster girl for Muslim or Asian women. At the time, many people would tell me, "You're a Muslim woman; you should speak up for Muslim and Asian women and focus your leadership development and coaching work on them." While I appreciated their sentiment, I didn't want to be limited to that role.

My first book, *Her Way to the Top*, resonated with women globally because it addressed the internal and external challenges women face, regardless of their background. I wanted my work to speak to women from all walks of life. But as time went on, I began to realise something important: I was—and always have been—proud to be a Muslim woman. However, I hadn't fully embraced or owned all the different facets of my identity in my work. I was just a career coach and trainer, broadly focusing on women's leadership without explicitly addressing my community.

That changed when I asked myself: *If I don't own my identity and speak up for the women in my community, then who will?* It was a turning point, driven by a deep sense of responsibility—especially as I witnessed the pervasive Islamophobia, racism, and xenophobia around me. What truly pushed me to act was the constant stream of negative stereotypes in the media about Muslim men and Pakistani men. For me, that narrative clashed with my reality. I've been surrounded by feminist men all my life—my grandfather, my father, and my husband are all incredible supporters of my work. I felt compelled to address those misconceptions and to amplify the voices and stories of Muslim women in particular.

That's when I began writing about these issues. I pitched several articles to the *Harvard Business Review*, and the one that finally got published was titled "How to Support Muslim Women." It went through over 100 edits because they had never published anything like it. When it finally came out, the impact was overwhelming. Women from across the globe reached out, sharing how they had felt the need to hide their Muslim identity or avoid speaking about it in the workplace. Reading the article gave them the confidence to discuss topics like employee resource groups and Muslim networks. That's when I realised how powerful my writing could be and how necessary it was for me to advocate for my community.

I've also been vocal about hijab bias. While I don't wear the hijab myself—and many women in my family don't either—we are all practising Muslims. For me, it's about defending the right to choose. It's about ensuring that women have the freedom to express themselves however they see fit. Over the past few years, I've been increasingly vocal about these issues, recognising that my voice can help make a difference.

Lisa You talked there about feminist Pakistani men, and as we speak, we're having this conversation at a time when politicians and the media are weaponising child sexual abuse to attend to the agenda of what many describe as "far right ideology." This ideological position is using child sexual exploitation and abuse to normalise a narrative about Muslim men. I can only imagine how hard it is to watch that as a Pakistani woman at the moment, as I personally, as a non-Muslim woman, find it horrendous.

Hira It's deeply frustrating, isn't it? Every time there's a terrorist attack, we're expected to denounce it—as though not doing so somehow publicly implies support. It's an absurd and offensive assumption to make about any decent human being.

The same goes for the issue of sexual exploitation or violence. Every single Pakistani Muslim man I know firmly condemns the vile actions of those who engage in such atrocities. They strongly believe in holding perpetrators accountable—without exception or allegiance based on shared ethnicity or faith.

What often gets overlooked is the fact that it was a British Pakistani Muslim man who demonstrated extraordinary courage and leadership—risking his own and his family's safety—to prosecute one of the most infamous grooming gangs. This example of moral conviction rarely makes the headlines in the same way the crimes do. Instead, we're subjected to far-right narratives that weaponise these cases to dehumanise, shame, and vilify an entire community.

The truth is that ethnicity should be irrelevant when it comes to prosecuting heinous criminals. What matters is justice for the victims. But let's not be naive—we see how ethnicity and faith are weaponised to unfairly target Black and Brown communities. Reopening certain investigations under the guise of delivering justice feels less about centring victims and more about perpetuating a political agenda. This serves to demonise already marginalised communities, while re-traumatising victims.

Yes, we unequivocally support justice for the victims. But we refuse to be baited into race-based narratives designed to incite division or paint a false picture of our faith. Islam, at its core, condemns all forms of injustice, harm, and exploitation—irrespective of the victim's background. We will not allow the actions of a few to define entire communities, and we reject the deliberate distortion of our values and beliefs.

What's also hurtful is how some non-Pakistani Asian men are quick to say, "Oh, it's just Pakistani men," as though distancing themselves somehow absolves them or makes them morally superior. It shifts the blame, and it's incredibly damaging.

As a Muslim feminist writer, I find this balance to be precarious. On one hand, I want to hold my community accountable and call out what's wrong. On the other, I'm acutely aware that anything I say can be weaponised to fuel Islamophobia, racism, and xenophobia. It's a double-edged sword. How do you speak out in a way that holds perpetrators accountable without allowing your words to be twisted into ammunition against an entire community?

The reality is we're not silent—we're measured. We're mindful of the consequences of our words in a world that's all too ready to misconstrue them. For us, it's not just about speaking out; it's about doing so responsibly, knowing the stakes are high for the people we're trying to protect.

Lisa In your writing around Muslim women in the workplace, what did you find?

Hira There's a persistent media bias when it comes to Muslim women, rooted in this Western stereotype that a woman can either be a feminist or a Muslim—but not both. This fuels a harmful narrative about "poor Muslim women" or "oppressed Muslim women" who supposedly need rescuing. These reductive and pejorative labels, such as "subservient Asian women," strip Muslim women of their individuality and agency.

During COVID-19, this bias became even more evident. The media frequently used images of Muslim women in hijabs or niqabs alongside stories about the virus. Why? What's the relevance? Were they implying that Muslim women were responsible for spreading COVID? Because that's the correlation many would subconsciously draw—"Muslims are careless," "Muslims are the problem." It was deliberate and damaging.

In fact, the media disproportionately focused on women in niqabs—a face-covering veil worn by a small minority of Muslim women (less than 1% across Europe)—to paint an image of "otherness." This visual cue subtly but powerfully suggested that Muslim women don't belong in British or Western culture. The reality is that many Muslim women, myself included, don't wear hijabs or niqabs, but the intent was clear: to make Muslim women appear alien and incompatible with the societies in which they live.

Note

- Niqab is a face-covering veil that leaves only the eyes visible, worn by a very small fraction of Muslim women.
- Hijab is a headscarf that covers the hair, neck, and sometimes shoulders, leaving the face visible. It's a more commonly worn form of modest dress among Muslim women.

What frustrates me further is the harmful dichotomous binary created between "good Muslims" and "bad Muslims." This narrative often portrays liberal Muslims as the "good ones" while practising Muslims are cast as backward or extreme. But there's no such thing as a "good

Muslim" versus a "bad Muslim." A more accurate distinction would be "practising" and "non-practising." These simplistic labels overlook the complexity of Muslim identities and experiences, forcing people into narrow boxes that don't reflect reality.

As a practising Muslim who doesn't wear a hijab, I've seen how these stereotypes are weaponised against us, creating division and fuelling Islamophobia. It's crucial that we challenge these harmful narratives and demand more nuanced, accurate representations of Muslim women in the media.

Lisa What are the things that can make a real difference in the workplace?

Hira Simple things like prayer spaces, make sure that people have spaces where they can pray. These are small things, avoiding faith, stereotyping, challenging media's role in shaping these unrealistic and limited perceptions of Muslims and also recognising that Muslims are a diverse group. They represent various ethnicities, backgrounds, and countries. So avoiding making assumptions based on appearances or attire.

Acknowledging that personal choices such as wearing a hijab are individual preferences rather than something imposed is helpful. I also think that designing inclusive networking opportunities because often Muslim women and even Muslim men miss out on a lot of opportunities after work because he said I don't drink. So thankfully, I think people are now focusing on having inclusive events, paying attention to dietary needs, dietary practices, choosing venues with various food options and also labelling them. I've been to venues and peeled apart sandwiches to see whether this is chicken or egg or tuna.

Making these little things will really help Muslim women and men attend the events comfortably. It doesn't have to be something elaborate. It's basic. Just ask them before they attend lunches or dinners, do you have any dietary requirements? I recently went to an event, and delivered a keynote at the Royal Navy, which was really nice. They knew I wasn't drinking and they kept on bringing these amazingly delicious nonalcoholic concoctions, which were amazing. They were so good. They were delicious. I've never had them before, but then I went to another event. People were being served exotic drinks, red wine and white wine; when I said I don't drink, there was no alternative and literally, they brought me water, but what, can I not have fancy drinks?

Lisa As someone who doesn't drink, I totally hear you!

Hira Simple adjustments can go a long way in creating an inclusive environment for Muslims. For example, providing prayer spaces is a small but meaningful step. It ensures that people of faith can practise their religion comfortably at work or events.

Another critical area is avoiding faith-based stereotyping. The media plays a massive role in shaping limited and often negative perceptions of Muslims. But it's important to challenge these biases and recognise that Muslims are not a monolith. We come from diverse ethnicities, backgrounds, and countries, and personal choices—like wearing a hijab—are individual preferences, not mandates.

Networking opportunities are another area where inclusivity is crucial. Many Muslim women and men miss out on after-work events because they don't drink alcohol. Thankfully, there's growing awareness about hosting inclusive events, but more can be done. Paying attention to dietary needs is essential, like choosing venues with various halal options and labelling them clearly. I've been to events where I had to peel apart sandwiches to figure out if they contained chicken, egg, or tuna. These small changes can make a big difference.

When the Royal Navy thoughtfully served delicious nonalcoholic drinks at the keynote I gave recently, it made me feel seen and included. Offering nonalcoholic versions of cocktails shows consideration—it's such a small thing but incredibly impactful.

Building cultural awareness is equally important, especially in breaking the damaging stereotypes about Muslims that have persisted since 9/11. Promoting religious literacy in the workplace is key. Educate employees about Islam and, if needed, bring in guest speakers or managers from your organisation to share their insights.

These aren't grand gestures—they're basics. But they create a more inclusive environment where Muslims, whether men or women, can fully participate and feel respected.

Lisa What is it that you think organisations don't understand about Islamophobia?

Hira Many don't understand how these experiences feel like *death by a thousand cuts.* Recent news, such as the coverage of grooming gangs, may seem inconsequential to some, but for Pakistani or Muslim men, it's deeply damaging. Imagine going to work with the fear that colleagues might perceive you as a groomer or abuser simply because of your identity. It chips away at psychological safety.

Psychological safety is especially crucial given global events, like the conflict in Palestine, which has made Muslim colleagues feel unsafe about expressing themselves, just as Jewish colleagues may feel vulnerable. It's difficult to vocalise your advocacy or grief when the atmosphere doesn't feel supportive. Similarly, when a terrorist attack happens, the first thought many Muslims have isn't just grief for the victims, but also dread: "*I hope it wasn't a Muslim.*" This reflects the broader societal pressure of being collectively blamed for individual acts.

As a writer, I've faced this toll firsthand. The comments I received on my articles often targeted my faith and identity, saying vile things about Islam and Prophet Muhammad. My husband eventually asked me to stop reading them for my mental health. I've written about topics like prayer bans in schools or arranged marriages to counter misconceptions, but the pushback underscores the need for greater cultural awareness.

Take arranged marriages, for example. They're often misunderstood. I'm in an arranged marriage with my husband, but it's also a love marriage. Arranged doesn't mean forced. This cultural nuance is often missed because it doesn't align with certain Western norms, but that doesn't make it wrong.

Muslims globally are also grappling with the collective trauma of genocides and persecution—in Gaza, the Uyghur crisis in China, and beyond. The weight of these tragedies affects mental health deeply. Compassion and awareness can make a difference.

Small acts of understanding, like respecting Ramadan, go a long way. Most Muslims don't ask for favours, but avoiding events during iftar or acknowledging the month of fasting shows thoughtfulness. Similarly, showing respect for holidays, offering compassion, and fostering religious literacy in workplaces can create a more inclusive environment.

By addressing these small but significant actions, we can better support colleagues and create spaces where they feel safe, seen, and valued.

Lisa Yes, and if we're thinking about the benefits of organiations understanding the impact of Islamophobia, and working hard towards mitigating those impacts, then the rewards are huge. I've been to Pakistan several times and I know the kindness, the generosity, and the hospitality of Pakistani people. For me, I would feel deeply sad there, if that was not enjoyed because of misunderstandings of Muslim culture, Pakistan, and Islamophobia.

Hira There's a prevalent misconception that Muslim women are universally oppressed, but Islam granted rights to women over 1,400 years ago—rights that many societies only recently adopted. Muslim women were given the right to vote, propose marriage, and seek divorce. They have the right to inherit property that is entirely theirs, with no obligation to share it with their family. A Muslim woman's earnings are her own, while her husband is obligated to provide for her and the family.

These teachings showcase balance and respect, yet they're rarely highlighted. For instance, the Prophet Muhammad exemplified allyship in his time by actively supporting his wives—helping with household chores, taking out the rubbish, and embodying a spirit of partnership that modern allyship campaigns often promote.

The media, however, tends to present a one-dimensional narrative, leaving out these empowering aspects of Islam and the lived experiences of Muslim women. Organisations can counter these stereotypes and promote a more inclusive culture by fostering cultural literacy and allyship within workplaces.

People often question why women receive a smaller share of inheritance compared to men in Islamic law. The reason is that women are not obligated to share their inheritance, whereas men are responsible for supporting their parents, children, and siblings with their share. A woman's inheritance is entirely hers, while a man's share comes with familial obligations.

Similarly, the topic of four marriages in Islam is frequently misunderstood and misrepresented. It's important to highlight that this allowance comes with strict conditions and significant caveats. Historically, 1,400 years ago, during times of war, the Prophet permitted multiple marriages as an act of protection for widows and vulnerable women, ensuring they were not left destitute or at risk of harm. It wasn't about lust or personal indulgence—it was a social responsibility.

Even today, Islam's allowance for multiple marriages is not a blanket approval. The Quran explicitly requires absolute fairness in the treatment of all wives, including equal financial provision and emotional care. Realistically, it's nearly impossible for an ordinary person to meet these criteria. If you can't ensure complete fairness, the Quran advises to marry only one. This isn't just a recommendation—it's a directive designed to prevent harm and injustice.

Unfortunately, some people cherry-pick religious teachings to suit their narrative, often ignoring the full context and accompanying responsibilities. This isn't unique to Islam; similar misinterpretations occur in other religious texts, such as the Torah or the Bible. Addressing these misconceptions and understanding religious principles holistically is crucial rather than twisting them to justify personal desires or agendas.

When organisations commit to understanding and addressing Islamophobia, they foster an environment where employees feel safe, respected, and empowered. This doesn't just benefit Muslim colleagues—it enriches the workplace as a whole by tapping into diverse perspectives, enhancing collaboration, and driving innovation.

Lisa A lot of what we're talking about here is about education. It's about taking time to learn something from somebody else from another culture. But more than that, it's also about understanding the impact of what it does to a person to experience.

Hira There's a prevalent anti-Muslim sentiment that manifests in damaging stereotypes and narrow perceptions. I can't tell you how often I've heard comments like, "Oh, but you're a very empowered Muslim," or assumptions that the men in my family somehow hold me back. Why would they? My experience has been the opposite. The men in my family—my grandfather, father, brother, and husband—have always encouraged and supported me in everything I do.

In fact, the women in my family are a testament to empowerment and achievement. They are doctors, cardiologists, lawyers, anaesthesiologists, physicians, and even police officers. Women in my family work, thrive, and contribute meaningfully to society. Yet these realities are rarely acknowledged or reflected in mainstream narratives.

The media plays a huge role in twisting these stories, perpetuating a singular, distorted image of Muslim women as oppressed or powerless. As a result, people often fail to look beyond the surface, accepting these narrow portrayals as truth.

It's crucial to challenge these stereotypes and broaden understanding. By sharing authentic stories and lived experiences, we can dismantle harmful assumptions and foster a more inclusive and accurate representation of Muslim communities. This shift isn't just necessary—it's long overdue.

Lisa Thank you. You've been very generous in sharing from your work and your writing and how this can be applied to the workplace and caring for people who care.

Reflection

There are many things that can be implemented into the workforce that can make a significant difference, but as Hira explains, they are active and intentional, as with all things that are about cultivating belonging. They won't happen on their own. This chapter is timely with the continued and rising Islamophobic attitudes in the UK, in Europe, and in the US.

Discussion Points

1. **Psychological Safety and Islamophobia**
   - How psychologically safe do Muslim staff feel within my workplace or team?
   - Have I reflected on how microaggressions or subtle exclusions may impact the emotional well-being of Muslim colleagues?
2. **Recognising and Addressing Islamophobia**
   - What steps can I take to actively challenge Islamophobic assumptions or comments when I hear them?

- How do I support Muslim colleagues in expressing their concerns or experiences without fear of judgement or dismissal?

3. **Representation and Media Influence**
   - What are some misconceptions I may hold about Islam that I need to unlearn or investigate more deeply?
   - In what ways can I counteract harmful narratives by promoting more accurate and respectful representations?

4. **Media Bias Towards Muslim Women**
   - How can I challenge the stereotype that Muslim women are oppressed or lack autonomy?
   - Have I considered how workplace policies and behaviours might unintentionally perpetuate these stereotypes?

5. **Workplace Inclusivity and Cultural Literacy**
   - What small, inclusive changes can I or my organisation make to better accommodate Muslim staff (e.g. prayer spaces, meeting times)?
   - Do I feel confident in my knowledge of Islamic practices and how they relate to daily life, such as fasting or prayer?

6. **How is cultural and religious literacy embedded into our staff training or professional development opportunities?**
   - Am I showing allyship through action, such as advocating for religious accommodations or calling out bias?
   - Do I demonstrate understanding and empathy during important religious periods like Ramadan or Eid?

7. **The Impact of Stereotyping on Identity and Belonging**
   - Have I considered how stereotyping affects the sense of belonging for Muslim colleagues within the workplace?
   - How can I create and promote spaces where all individuals, regardless of faith or background, feel seen, valued, and respected?

8. **What ongoing actions am I taking to educate myself about Islam, Islamophobia, and the lived experiences of Muslim communities?**

- How can I ensure that anti-Islamophobia practice remains a consistent and integrated part of my professional and personal development, rather than a one-off response to incidents?
- What ongoing actions am I taking to educate myself about Islam, Islamophobia, and the lived experiences of Muslim communities?

Notes

1 The United States Agency for International Development was an independent US government organisation. Its work was to provide help for countries in need. It was established in 1961 by President John F Kennedy.
2 https://www.theguardian.com/us-news/2025/feb/10/trump-buy-gaza-plan.
3 https://www.politico.eu/article/mapped-europe-far-right-government-power-politics-eu-italy-finalnd-hungary-parties-elections-polling/.

9
A Conversation With Jane Hinchliffe
Decolonising the Workplace

This chapter highlights the importance of structural and behavioural changes in creating an inclusive and supportive environment. It acknowledges the complexity of decolonising work and emphasises the need for a solid foundation of knowledge and passion in the individuals involved.

Lisa What work are you engaged in, Jane?

Jane I work for a large further education group and I'm the Relational Practice Lead. I manage a very small team and really what we're about is culture change. Moving a big organisation from more traditional behaviourist approaches towards a more relational, trauma-informed culture. I feel that this way of doing things means we are by nature moving toward a more decolonised model. We want to make sure that people are able to come to college and turn up in the best way possible feeling safe, authentic, and understood.

    I recently completed a master's in Race Education and Decolonial Thought. I bring that with me in terms of

	thinking about how we can do things in a more trauma-informed and decolonised way in the workplace.
Lisa	When you're thinking about decolonisation and trauma-informed practice in a further education setting, what does that look like?
Jane	I feel like I am still learning what that looks like, and probably always will be. I believe none of us exist in any organisation that isn't influenced by the colonial legacy or a racialised society and we're all conditioned in a particular way. I'm really interested in the sociological theory of Omi and Winant (1994) on racial formation. So as I understand it, the idea that as part of becoming socialised we learn to see race and this affects everything and underpins everything. That race is socially constructed rather than biologically fixed, and that this lens we are socialised into affects how we judge others and behave towards them as individuals on conscious and subconscious levels and also on a systemic level. This way of viewing the world in which colonialism underpins everything is a type of thinking that exists at the core of organisations and institutions. So given the oppression is baked into our institutions, it is so important that we are aware of race trauma.

The traditional modes of discipline, which involve punishment, blame, shame, and guilt and the race binaries and white supremacy were all aspects of colonisation. So changing the way we think about discipline and behaviour feels both trauma informed and like part of a process of decolonising.

Critical Whiteness studies teach us the closer you are to that white ideal which is the profile of a person who is male, straight, cisgendered, nondisabled, financially successful, upper class, the more civilised you are perceived to be, and the better you're treated in society (or the more you can get away with). So this doesn't just impact on people who are racialised as Black. It impacts on all of us in different ways depending on our different lived experiences and varied identities. From this perspective, understanding this and accepting it, and taking a trauma-informed and intersectional (Crenshaw) approach to changing this has to be good for those of us who don't occupy the greatest levels of power in society, which is the majority.

If you think about the amount of blame, shame, and guilt we use in workplaces, and the judgement people often feel, this disproportionately affects people who are not racialised as white, and / or where you might have a range of struggles and protected characteristics in your lived experience that are not understood. The effect of all this can be reduced by using a trauma-informed approach with employees, our learners, and our customers across our individual behaviour, our processes and our systems. This would benefit everyone, and probably increase productivity, creativity, and well-being too. So where there is pushback, I think, for what reason? Is it that people at the top don't want to yield and hand over some of the power to move towards a less hierarchical structure perhaps? Is it that no one wants to put the time and energy into such a big change if they feel they are benefiting in some way from the status quo?

For me I feel that decolonising and being trauma informed should go hand in hand. An environment where it is ok to make mistakes, where there is collaboration and discussion around policies to benefit everyone, flatter, fairer wage structures, sharing of power and altering the senior management dynamics, fair boundaries and expectations, processes that are inclusive of a range of cultural and practical needs, self-education, and training around oppression and how it works to raise your own knowledge is a long way off for most organisations I would say. All these things are present in the six principles of Trauma-Informed Practice. I worry that a lot of the time we box tick in terms of being "Trauma Informed" in society as much as we box tick around matters of equality and equity.

I feel like binary thinking contributes to the problems, and colonial notions of what is civilised or acceptable or what is the "right way" to do something. A small example we use at work, which is not by any means changing the world but is a tangible example that I can give, is that for our training, we always sit in circles. We talk about links back to pre-colonial practices and the value of circles in a range of different indigenous cultures and why. So that we are crediting that practice and locating it where it began. Not to say all pre-colonial practices were perfect, just the idea of bringing some of that more ancient knowledge into the workplace rather than colonial ideas.

Lisa Indigenous wisdom.

Jane Yes. I guess also I'm wanting the workplace to soften a little bit. Yet often, how that gets misconstrued is if we soften, we won't have any boundaries. Actually, in terms of practicing in a trauma-informed way, we do need to have boundaries as well. People need to know where the edges are to feel safe. We're not getting rid of boundaries. Getting to know people really well and thinking about what might be influencing them and what they might be bringing with them. I have always found that a better way to work.

When I started my career I was in the private sector. I was really puzzled by this whole, "why haven't you done this?" and "this needs to be on my desk by this time or else." I remember getting shouted at and sworn at and also receiving emails in capital letters. Whilst that's quite an extreme example, in most workplaces there is a level of lack of psychological safety. I feel like, only a very small number of people can survive in that environment. A lot of people with bags of potential don't thrive in those sorts of environments. The level of change we need feels huge.

Lisa What sort of responses do you receive when you talk about decolonisation?

Jane I think often people are perplexed. Some people are starting to think about it more. I accept it's a journey and I think many of us are at different points on the journey or refusing to go in that direction of travel altogether. For example, in terms of doing discipline differently, some people respond by enforcing the status quo from the view of "this is the way it's always worked" and "it's always worked fine for me, so why would you change it?" I have worked in many educational settings over the years, and there is definitely a range of thinking from professionals. Some people have very strong evidence to support high-discipline approaches. For example, they'll talk about getting students to stand up for the rest of the lesson when there has been talking, shouting at young people in front of their peers using shame, and appearing surprised when the person responds negatively to this (wouldn't you?) or taking away social time when that is often a time young people use to emotionally regulate or decompress, or sending a student home for wearing the wrong uniform (in schools) when they may have struggled to attend for several weeks.

Lisa They were all made to stand up for the rest of the lesson?

Jane Yes. These stories are often followed up with "well it worked" or "they never misbehaved again." Or "consistency is very important." Some express shock that a young person was rude in response to one of these approaches.

So when the argument is made that the approach "worked"—did it really? In the short term or the long term? What did the person learn from that and what did you model about how to treat other human beings? How is that now affecting their learning and their feelings about you, which also impact on their learning? I guess some people feel quite threatened by letting go of these ways of coping as well.

Given that these disciplinarian approaches will disproportionately impact on anyone noticed more because, for example, they are racialised as Black and being negatively profiled, we have to be mindful of why, with a trauma-informed lens, anti-racist lens, challenging the status quo and rooting out our own harmful thinking is so important. We need to have some pretty bold conversations about who you are telling off and why and are you misreading their behaviour because of your own prejudicial thinking (for example stereotyping of young Black males or females as aggressive, perceiving Black young people to be older than they are, responding with less empathy). Also train staff to notice different types of struggles and ways of seeking communication through behaviour, and to reflect on who they are not noticing and why.

Lisa I'm interested in this sense of being threatened by this culture shift and lens through which to see the world we're living in. It's work that's about changing the status quo.

Jane Yes.

Lisa Trauma-informed practice, until more recently, very much aroused threat for many. It's challenging and it's asking people to see the world very differently. I think we've made great strides in this area across all the sectors. It was a very different experience in my area of work even going back to the beginning of the decade commencing in 2010. Shifting the dial further into thinking about decolonisation is invariably going to be very challenging and yet such an integral aspect of trauma-informed practice. I'm currently reading *Hospicing Modernity* (Machado de Oliveira [2021]), which spends at least the first three chapters warning people that they're going to be challenged, that if they don't want to do the work to not read the rest of the book so there is an anticipation already that doing this work going to activate a reaction.

Jane Yes. In terms of the interpersonal anti-racism aspect of this, I think a lot of that is defensiveness you get can be very hard to manage. What seems to have happened in the workplace is that there's been a level of awareness around unconscious bias; whenever you talk about racism, people bring up unconscious bias and what they've learned about microaggressions. They will often express that they think that this learning is really important and "I know not to do it now; I didn't know I was doing it before." I think this training can lead people to feel that the job's done. There are two main issues I see here which came out as part of my study. Firstly, perhaps we are doing a bit of self-reflection, but what are we doing to challenge the status quo in the workplace when we see entrenched, systemic discrimination?

Secondly, one person becoming aware of their bias and what a microaggression is doesn't mean they would spot or understand every racial microaggression or behave better. If you are from a white background, you will miss it. So you need to get into a place where you are willing to accept feedback graciously, think carefully before speaking, and unlearn some of your conditioning in order to make progress to reduce your interpersonal racism. What happens in reality is that we often don't do this, and we get into thinking our intention equals our impact. Whether we mean it or not, it might've upset somebody. We need to get better at accepting when we are challenged and resisting the urge to react with anger, tears, or victimhood. Otherwise we go round in circles.

A bit of history that shapes this in relation to white women for example—when you go back to colonialism, white women were positioned as virtuous. They went with their husbands to the colonies and they were seen as civilising in those colonies. An interesting quote form Ware (2015) highlights this:

The Englishwoman abroad could be at once a many-faceted figure: from an intrepid adventuress defying racial and sexual boundaries to heroic mother responsible for the preservation of the white "race"; from the devoted missionary overseeing black souls to the guardian of white morals; from determined pioneer and companion to the white man to a vulnerable, defenceless piece of his property.

(p. 131)

Depictions of white women as virtuous have endured to a degree. So we link our behaviour to our belief in our own inherent virtue, therefore we can never be racist. We understand racism to be violent acts from, say, the far right and we don't accept our own everyday mistakes as a form of everyday racism.

Occasionally, a person can graciously accept when they might have got something wrong. Generally, we are so alarmed by the idea of being unintentionally racist that we can't accept it. This means it is not psychologically safe to challenge us and we go round in circles causing more harm. We need to build our resilience to getting something wrong, being challenged, and learning from it.

Lisa   This reminds me of the Johari window as well. It's the things that you can't see that other people can see.

Lisa   So how might that be approached?

Jane   My research highlighted different schools of thought on how to approach interpersonal racism. For example, one

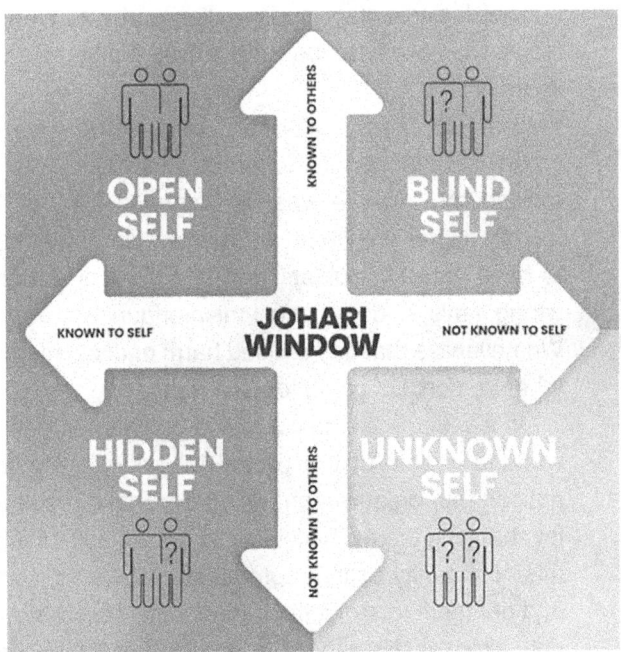

Figure 9.1   Johari Window.

way is we want to get away from cancel culture, this stuff where people feel they can't ask questions for fear of repercussions. They need to feel safe to make mistakes and we need to set that environment. But that's very much centring the person who is causing the harm.

Another is people who identify as white, like me, need to take more responsibility than this. The information about discrimination and structural discrimination has been around for years. There are hundreds of really accessible books, online resources, stuff on TikTok if you genuinely want to understand WHAT needs to change. There is a level of taking personal responsibility for our learning. If organisations are trying to create the type of environment where it is ok to make mistakes, it needs to be safe for people of the Global Majority to challenge without facing unfair recrimination and a turning of the tables where the person who caused the harm is framed as the victim.

From a trauma-informed perspective, we need to be helping people to feel comfortable with being challenged because what is triggering for them? Why is it so distressing? Part of my own journey is learning to have broad shoulders and say "I'm sorry. I got that wrong. I misgendered you. I mispronounced your name." Whatever it is that has caused harm or discomfort for the other person. I'm going to put it right.

On a wider scale, policies and procedures that disadvantage people of the Global Majority are sometimes noticed, but organisations often don't take responsibility for changing them. The focus is often on, ask people from this community or that community what is going wrong and get them to suggest changes. Suggestions are then not taken on board. There is plenty documented evidence what's going wrong and the problems are in the system. So why are we refusing to look at the information that is already out there and asking the same questions over again, to then discount the advice that is given?

The information and the evidence has been there for years. If you're not going to respond to it now, why should a person of colour use their emotional labour to educate you? And why should people be working to make the changes more palatable for people in power?

And I think what happens is, in the workplace, a lot of the time we have these initiatives that teach people about unconscious biases, very light touch, but nothing really changes, it just ticks a box for the Equality, Diversity, and Inclusion (EDI) agenda.

Lisa Power is intrinsic in this conversation from every angle; it's multilayered because in order to manage challenge you have to feel safe and you have to feel safe to be challenged so that you can be vulnerable enough to say "I got that wrong, I'm so grateful that you've taken the time to talk to me about how you felt" and what we're really talking about here is power and seeking to mitigate the impact of racial trauma.

Jane Yes.

Lisa Do you think that the practice of anti-racist allyship is helpful in tackling and reducing racial trauma?

Jane My dissertation for my master's degree was about *Deconstructing the Anti-Racist Ally* (Hinchliffe, 2022). Some of the people I interviewed were aiming to practice anti-racist allyship in the workplace, or they were people of Global Majority backgrounds trying to promote anti-racism and coming up against barriers. Some of them were in the workplace, some of them were in activism, obviously different spaces. Allyship is interesting because it seems to have emerged and become popular during a kind of very neoliberal backdrop and is very much a Global North (Western) and Americanised idea. The UK has adopted the concept and if you think about our cultures focusing very much on the individual, it has taken on a Westernised, individualised tone. So it's seen as individual work, challenging your own issues within, and looking at your privilege and acknowledging it.

From my research, I feel like you could argue that we've got stuck there. There's a lot of naval gazing and hand wringing going back to guilt and shame and white virtue. "I'm trying to be a good person. I've purged myself of this racism now." In one study, Delfino (2021) looked at racio linguistics in online spaces. There was a white woman asking her Black friends if she had ever caused them any microaggressions? She asked to have these explained to her so that she could make good and apologise. This seemed to this woman a very powerful thing to do. It seemed like she was absolutely centring herself and her need to be absolved in the discourse rather than focusing on any sort of meaningful, systemic change. Imagine the emotional labour of a Black or Brown person trying to have this conversation. It could be uncomfortable and possibly unsafe depending on her response. There was a massive disconnect there and an absence of trauma-informed thinking. So for me, I think it depends how allyship is framed, but my conclusion in the end was that allyship as a journey of an individual is not particularly effective.

Simply becoming aware of your privilege and avoiding microaggressions does not dismantle systemic racism. In terms of systemics I was having a conversation with someone about some safeguarding practices the other day and whether there was an awareness of anti-racism in safeguarding and protections for young people of the Global Majority from systemic and interpersonal oppression. People don't automatically consider anti-racism as a feature of safeguarding; yes, they talk about protected characteristics and vulnerabilities and how we need to bear those in mind, but it doesn't really go much further than that a lot of the time.

Lisa That's shocking.

Jane And the fact that we can sometimes either miss things or not intervene, going right back to Victoria Climbié, how much have things really changed? In terms of feeling comfortable and having the racial literacy to understand how we view children of the Global Majority and what they are experiencing differently, our misunderstandings of what we consider to be cultural practices, what's harmful, what isn't, how to challenge harm in an appropriate way, and also thinking about what it feels like as a Black or Brown person to work with social services where you will likely come up against all these things that could make the situation worse, not better—trust in services understandably remains low.

Victoria Climbié

The inquiry investigated the circumstances surrounding the tragic and horrific death of Victoria Climbié, who was murdered in February 2000 at the hands of her aunt and her boyfriend. An inquiry followed which was chaired by Lord Laming and the findings of that inquiry (the Laming Report) were damning, highlighting the failures of senior managers in various organisations and a resistance to accept responsibility for them.

Lisa It strikes me that there are so many routes out of really exploring anti-racism, that every time it comes to the fore, there's another road that can take people away from the issue at hand, an escape route if you like.

Jane Definitely. "Privilege" is a really interesting one. As one of the participants in my research pointed out, people conflate white privilege with financial privilege a lot of the time (Hinchliffe, 2022). So they'll say "I had a working class background and we didn't have money." You will still have had some privilege that comes with having white skin. But you didn't have class privilege or financial privilege.

But if you consider bell hook's idea that we live in an "Imperialist white supremacist capitalist patriarchy" (The Bell Hooks Centre, 2025, n.p.), if you look at it like that, the further you are away from that white ideal, the more you're going to struggle. If you're from a working-class background, if you're from an Irish background, if you're from any background, or have protected characteristics that means you are othered and treated slightly differently, you'll be slightly further away from that ideal.

We're not trying to say everyone's struggles are equal. But that most of us do have struggles within this system. And anyway, why would I be ok with any human being treated worse than me because they are racialised differently or working class or disabled or trans for example? From a purely selfish perspective if that's the one you want to take, if we make things better for people who are more marginalised, I believe it is going to benefit most of us, emotionally, spiritually, and in terms of well-being. Maybe some people in positions of power just don't want to let go of any financial privileges they have to create better well-being for everyone, and those who feel they are benefiting from the current system in some ways don't want it to change.

If we could all see the benefits of a more equitable society, including some of those men who are successful in the current system, because men have all this toxic masculinity thing to live up to in this system which harms them too, we could build some solidarity across all the different intersectional identities.

And then also just thinking about it in terms of how we build communities of practice. Just the idea of everyone coming together and talking about this, instead of arguing about one group getting more than another. The oppression is done to us by those in the higher echelons of power, and the systems they have created that we uphold, not by each other.

Lisa There are lots of "communities of practice" now, aren't there, around the trauma-informed practice space, which is really lovely.

So what are the main things that you would change if you were starting on this process and with the knowledge that you have now been on this process for a while, and you were advising somebody else? What areas would you say they really needed to focus on?

Jane I would ask people to, firstly, raise your awareness, link with a reputable consultant, and prepare the ground perhaps by getting your team to engage in anti-racist reading or learning in a suitable format for you, then talk more about the issues instead of avoiding them. Build some commitment and motivation within your team rather than just box ticking. Undertake proper in-depth anti-racism training with someone who has *both* lived experience of racism *and* expertise and a theoretical understanding of anti-racism and decolonial thought. Training should not be unconscious bias focused or solely focused on interpersonal racism. It's going to be hard at points and require you to unlearn, unpick things and make big changes.

You have to look at policies, procedures, and practices and think how we can make those different. So you would need a working group, to consider how to decolonise. In terms of intersectionality (Crenshaw) this is going to benefit anyone from any marginalised identity, and it is going to increase creativity, openness, and diversity of thought.

This approach ensures we are not singling Black or Brown staff members who are not interested in focusing on anti-racism and not making them feel like they need to be a spokesperson or an expert for everybody—which of course is really problematic.

I think we miss the mark when we don't understand that there's a theoretical basis to this work. It's not just about getting someone who you've known for years, who happens to be a person of Global Majority background to tell you what they think.

I would be looking at policies, procedures, and practices rather than focusing on individual aspects of behaviour. But in terms of individual aspects of behaviour, I'd be thinking about reflective practice, group sessions, and modelling how we behave when we're challenged and tackling how we feel when we're challenged.

In terms of processes and procedures they can be very centred around the white British perspective, and not suited to people from a range of marginalised groups either. We need to interrogate what we consider to be the correct way to do things. Often if you don't go through "the proper channels," you don't get anywhere. How many people get stuck at the bottom of the heap because they can't access these "proper channels"? Rethinking all of those processes in a way that makes them easy, convenient, and truly accessible to everybody. This is a massive, huge piece of work. It's not a small piece of work. So from that perspective, you can see why people just do a bit of unconscious bias training, then move on.

Lisa It's very similar to the trauma-informed practice as well and thinking about anti-racism for me is an integral part of trauma-informed practice anyway.

Jane You and I were in the same meeting recently and I was so happy to hear you speaking about racial trauma in the meeting because I'd not been to any of your training. I was really excited to hear that because not everybody involved in trauma-informed practice highlights it as much.

Lisa It's really interesting, but in Scotland, the trauma-informed principle, which is on gender and cultural, historical considerations, is not part of their Trauma-Informed Toolkit. For me, to remove gender and cultural, historical considerations out of the trauma-informed framework really shaves off a bulk of trauma-informed practice because of racial trauma and gender trauma.

Jane Yes. It seems like that route out, that avoidance that you mentioned before. Racial literacy is really lacking and people feel very afraid to talk about anything related to race and the legacies of history. If you look at Israel and Palestine for example people struggle to talk about it. It is possible to hold in mind those families that lost people in October and hostages, and Palestinians who are suffering, and losing loved ones as well. You can see that some of those policies that silence people talking about Palestinian suffering for fear of upsetting the Jewish community aren't clearly expressing how we can care about both groups and wish for safety and well-being for everyone in the region whether Jewish or Muslim. Yes, that's complex, but we can talk about it without discrimination towards either group.

We lack racial literacy, so I feel like that's why it gets missed off as in the Scotland example. We don't know how to talk about this and feel safe, or to handle any challenges to what we say, so we leave it out altogether. We need to have some conversations more, not less.

Lisa It's perceived as too difficult.

Jane Yeah, which is why I feel the idea of a racial formation (Omi and Winants) is so relevant. When you go back to Marx and you think about class and you think that class is the driver of everything I'm a bit conflicted with that because I feel the racial formation and colonialism drives capitalism, classism, and all the other prejudices against the full range of marginalised groups. Now, that's just my opinion, obviously, but I think it's really interesting. Yes, classism is a huge issue that gets overlooked all the time, but I feel there is more sympathy for it in the discourse about inequality than race. When race is mentioned people often moan and say all this focus on racism is ridiculous. But we don't focus on it. We just get angry and close down the conversation. People are afraid to seem racist, so instead of spending some time learning and acknowledging what needs to change, the conversations are avoided or get reduced to personal attacks or "whataboutary" and the ignorance around it continues.

Lisa The intersection between race and class is huge.

Jane Definitely, and between race and lots of other protected characteristics. And if we understood more we could do so much more for so many people, and I really think it would make healthier happier workplaces! I am always hoping for more progress and to see genuine motivation for change!

Reflection

The reader may feel a discomfort in reading this conversation. It forces a reflection within about what role we each have in contributing to dismantling racism and the colonial practices that pervade all of our services and education. For the reader racialised as white, the challenge is not to be frightened of that discomfort but rather to use it in ways that harness some kind of action for change.

Discussion Points

1. **Challenges and Conditions**
   - How has my own social conditioning shaped the way I view race, power, and authority in professional settings?
   - In what ways might traditional disciplinary methods I use reinforce colonial or racial binaries?
2. **Training and Pre-Colonial Practices**
   - How can I incorporate reflective, communal practices (like circle discussions) into my work to foster equity and collective engagement?
   - What can I learn from pre-colonial traditions, and how can I integrate this knowledge respectfully and critically?
3. **Defensiveness and Fragility**
   - When am I most likely to respond with defensiveness, and what might that reveal about my unconscious biases or privilege?
   - How can I hold space for the impact of my actions, even if the intent was not harmful?

4. **Privilege and Systemic Racism**
   - How do I understand privilege beyond wealth or access, and how does that affect my work with diverse communities?
   - In what ways am I actively contributing to dismantling systemic racism, rather than just avoiding offensive behaviour?
5. **Decolonising Policies and Practices**
   - What steps can I take to ensure that decolonising efforts in my workplace are more than symbolic gestures?
   - How can I participate in or support working groups aimed at decolonising our organisational practices?
6. **Paying for Expertise**
   - Do I value and compensate the lived experiences of people of colour equitably in professional settings?
   - How can I ensure that decolonising work is grounded in both lived experience and robust theoretical understanding?
7. **Focus on Policies, Procedures, and Practices**
   - Which organisational policies or procedures in my workplace reflect outdated or colonial thinking?
   - How can I contribute to modelling reflective, anti-oppressive responses in difficult or challenging situations?
8. **Support and Response to Challenges**
   - How do I respond when challenged about my language, actions, or assumptions—do I see it as an opportunity to grow?
   - What strategies can I use to challenge others constructively, without resorting to tone policing or deflecting discomfort?

References

Delfino, J. (2021). White allies and the semiotics of wokeness: Raciolinguistic chronotypes of white virtue on Facebook. *Journal of Linguistic Anthropology*, 31, 238–277.

Hinchliffe, J. (2022). *De-Constructing the Anti-Racist Ally; The Challenges, Benefits and Impacts of Allyship*. Unpublished—Leeds Beckett University Repository.

hooks, b. (2025). https://www.berea.edu/centers/the-bell-hooks-center, accessed on 16th March 2025.

Machado de Oliveira, V. (2021). *Hospicing Modernity: Facing Humanity's Wrongs and the Implications for Social Activism*. Berkeley, CA: North Atlantic Books.

Omi, M., & Winant, H. (1994). *Racial Formation in the United States*. London: Routledge.

Ware, V. (2015). *Beyond the Pale: White Women, Racism, and History*. 2nd ed. London: Verso.

10
A Conversation With Karen Treisman

Reflecting on Intergenerational and Ancestral Trauma

This section of the book invites us to think about trauma beyond our own individual experiences, moving us into considering trauma from the past, from the culture, from the community. With that in mind, it felt absolutely appropriate that I have a conversation with my friend and colleague, Dr Karen Treisman, on intergenerational and ancestral trauma.

Lisa   You have extensive experience in the field of trauma: collective, individual, and organisational. In that context, I'm interested in speaking to you about a couple of things. One of those is around intergenerational trauma and the other is on the subject of genocide and the impact that those things have on the workforce. So, I wonder if we can start with intergenerational trauma.

Karen   It's just so big and multilayered. It's such a huge area, isn't it? Because there are the parts around people in the workforce, who, for example, might have had parents who were in war, using drugs or alcohol, have been in the care system, who have been in prison, and so many others! So, there's so many different potential experiences people have faced and have had to navigate and adapt to, not just intergenerational trauma, but also ancestral, inherited, and historical trauma.

And I guess within this, when we think about aspects such as slavery, colonisation, systemic oppression, displacement, the refugee experience, we know that those patterns and imprints might have been transferred, passed on, or echoed through and within the generations, the haunters, ghosts, and angels and lights of the past. The possible reverberations, wounds, and legacy of trauma, hurt, pain, and suffering. Of course, there are so many textures, and for some people these might consciously have been named or shared, and that might be a really important part of their expressed narrative, identity, and self-story. For others, it might be much less known, spoken about, understood, or more held in the background and backdrop of their life or identity. There are also so many pathways and levels from the passing on biologically, physiologically, and from an epigenetic perspective—through the parenting, attachment, family dynamics, the stories we hear and are marinated by, and so much more!

The ways that this might filter into the workplace are so vast and nuanced, but I guess an everyday example might be, and of course, there are multiple interplaying factors, so I'm not saying all intergenerational trauma, but might be, for example, how we might respond to criticism or feedback, or feeling judged for our experience to making "mistakes" or being silenced or ignored at work. This might be entangled and influenced by our relationship, history, and experience previously to, for instance, being ignored, being belittled, not feeling heard, made to feel less than etc. Similarly, to key aspects in work, like our relationship in groups (our first group was a family), or our history and experience to and with authority, and how that might play out or be activated or resurfaced in our relationship with our manager/ supervisor etc.

Another example might be around people's relationship to security and stability, or how an unpredictable work environment might feel, or if there is a big restructure or change in the organisation, or aspects around our relationship to emotional expression, or to asking for help; the list goes on and on.

Note

Intergenerational trauma refers to the transmission of the effects of trauma from individuals who have experienced it directly to subsequent generations. This transmission can occur through various mechanisms, including genetic, psychological, and familial interactions (Yehuda & Lehrner, 2018).

Multigenerational trauma encompasses the cumulative psychological and emotional effects that trauma experienced by one generation can have on subsequent generations within a family or community (Sotero, 2006).

Historical trauma is cumulative emotional and psychological wounding over the lifespan and across generations, emanating from massive group trauma experiences (Brave Heart, 2003).

Lisa When we're working with people who have similar experiences that we may have had, that can bring to the fore different things that an organisation might not want to deal with. There are times when being "activated" by something we're working with is unavoidable. Something has unconsciously been "tapped into" and when people are unaware that this is part of the work, this can cause all sorts of difficulties. In your experience of working organisationally, what practices have you seen that are good and what practices have you seen that are not so good?

Karen I think you're absolutely right in terms of if you take a social worker, as an example, it might be the work that they're doing understandably might remind that person of their own family or of their own dynamics, or it might be more subtle and more cryptic. For example, the situation might make the person feel not listened to, and this feels thorny, as it might be reminiscent of other situations where one has felt not listened to or respected. Someone might have a conscious recollection of this, but very often it will be more imprinted on a deeper level, and the person just has a response. Or, for example, in an organisational context, their manager might make them feel criticised or shamed, and that might stir or activate something in previous experiences. That might take them down a memory or a feeling time hole to other times that they might have felt that. So, what is happening in the "here and now" can be entangled with what happened in the "there and then." For example, someone might feel that a decision has been made that is unfair and unjust, and this might understandably feel even more heightened and intensified if it taps into our own values, principles, or past experiences of having things happen that were unfair or unjust. Often when we don't know why these things are happening or there is not time to understand or to be curious or remember that we don't have an emotional X-ray or how trauma can show up, it can be puzzling, confusing, scary, and sometimes the person can be positioned as "overreacting, being too sensitive, being reactive, blowing out of proportion" and so forth. And in a work situation, this might lead to further mistrust or tension in the relationship.

I guess with best practice, the work is thorny and often there is a lot of emotional heavy lifting. So, we need organisations to see people as humans first, and not as a "them and us" but as a "we." Trauma is widespread, common, and prevalent, and most people come into this type of work for a reason. The more the impact of the work and the embodied experiences and wisdoms people bring are named, validated, made space for, acknowledged, and anticipated, the better—if done with care and respect. Of course this takes courage, openness, humility, and bravery and there needs to be psychological safety. This will look and feel different in different organisations. But in essence, so much of trauma has happened in secret; there has been a conspiracy of silence, often shame, denial, and pushed under the carpet. That is where it is "safe" to do so, having an acknowledgement and a torch shone on it is important. Even if not directly, but to have a shared sense of humanity, to be people first, and to have language to name and think about these things, such as around intergenerational trauma and understanding the possible patterns, ripples, and echoes of trauma feels important. James Baldwin said, "Not everything faced can be changed but nothing that isn't faced can be changed."

I also think there needs to be a menu of options, as no one size fits all, and we know often it is not what is on offer, but the nuances of how it is offered, and how it lands, and who it is offered by etc. And what works or fits one person won't fit another, or at a different time. But I have seen beautiful examples of spaces of solidarity, cultural affinity groups, healing circles, thinking spaces, and reflective practice. In essence, spaces where people feel seen, heard, believed, welcomed, valued, and listened to. Also, depending on the relationship having amazingly supportive and enriching discussions in supervision, and I mean "Super Vision" not "snoopervision." I also think having respectful workshops and training on aspects of organisational stress and trauma, compassionate fatigue, moral injury, activist burnout, our own role within the work and the work culture, our own well-being, how we regulate, and anchor can be incredibly helpful in creating spaces for these things to be named and to create a shared language. They also can make it feel less personal and can support people to viewing these things as occupational hazards and some of the costs of caring, and support people to maybe recognise what can happen without having to dive in too quickly about their own responses.

Another best practice I think is having support for leaders and managers on having thorny conversations and being able to hold space, but also, to understand how the work might push on tender or emotional ouch spots. And of course, if we can't do that, to try to minimise or avoid things that might add harm, like ignoring, pushing under the carpet, telling or conveying things like "Don't cry over spilt milk, toughen up, soldier on, get on with it" etc. We know these positions, said or felt, can be invalidating, minimising, and further silence these needs; then they are likely to spill or leak out in other ways. And there needs to be an acknowledgement that you as Lisa Cherry or me as Karen Treisman might work with the same person, but our own beliefs and experiences are going to shape and influence how we show up, our energy, our filter, our lens, what might be painful, what might be wounding, what we might pay more attention to, or less attention to. So, I think a lot of it is around actually first realising, recognising, and acknowledging. Which fits with the trauma-informed workplace culture, of being curious instead of furious. Recognising how these things might show themselves. Realising how they might be visiting or impacting. And reflecting on what might be happening for people and the organisation, whilst being mindful that we don't have emotional X-rays and we often don't need to know what someone's experiences have been, but can still hold it in mind as a possibility and so be honouring and respectful that it might have. It is like I often say in training, we might be sitting in, for example, a meeting in social services, and whilst everyone is talking about that child in care, or that mum on drugs, or that such and such dad, how do you know that several social workers in that room might also have been in care, or have or been a mum on drugs, and so forth. It is not us and them. And so, we need to walk gently and respectfully in the lives of others. That fits with the universal approach of trauma informed.

Lisa I'm always reminding people that in that universal approach, we don't need to know what people have experienced but if we work in a trauma-informed way, we have less chance of adding to harm and a greater opportunity to open up a healing space.

Karen Exactly. A few other examples of best practice could be separate books in themselves! In addition to the validating and normalising, fostering and trying to increase moral, psychological, and cultural safety within the workplace culture are so important. Infusing and embedding trauma-informed values can really help with improving things like trust and communication. Widening the lens of "trauma" so it includes the broader aspects of things like intergenerational trauma, systemic oppression, genocide, and so much more. Naming and acknowledging historical injustices and how different people might have been affected and impacted (not once but in an ongoing infusion of conversations). Thinking about how well-being is infused throughout the process including in recruitment and induction. Putting things in place to have meaningful and personalised healing and well-being plans which are more than a tick box exercise. Having access to training and support for understanding these concepts but also having tangible things that people can do to stay in the work, both micro dosing that can be infused throughout the day. Spaces to decompress or take our brains and nervous systems to the gym. As well as more long-term plans.

Some people might find things like coaching, mentoring, as shared before healing circles, but again, there shouldn't be an assumption as there needs to be choice within this. And there is a lot about organisational healing practices and around collective and community care.

Lisa And if we don't have those kinds of policies and procedures . . . you're describing an environment where it's safe and where there are relationships. And I was reminded of something while you were speaking. It's no accident that this is the chapter where I stray into the personal with ease, because I'm talking to you, Karen, and we know each other very well. I remember and I have written about this before, I remember when I moved a young person with their belongings in bin bags and in that moment, I remembered that experience myself as a child. It took my breath away. I remember thinking to myself, "I'm not going to think about that ever again."

I was in my early 20s, and I just thought I'm not going to think about that ever again. It was too close, too raw, and there was not one person at that workplace that I felt I could even vaguely unpick this with.

If you're working in a very authentic way in an environment where you have safe and authentic relationships that recognise that we are all human and we are all bringing *something*, then the opportunities are present to notice. It is intentional. Those relationships and the spaces they are nurtured in don't happen by accident.

Karen I so hear you and thanks for sharing that. It is painful and can linger and shape and stay with you. When you have that jellyfish zap moment. And the difference that would have potentially happened if you had been held in mind, if someone noticed, or if you had the impact acknowledged, had someone be curious, checked in with you, given permission messages, or given you support in that moment or what would have made it feel safer to be able to share. The other side of it, which I suppose both me and you massively advocate for, as shared before a bit, is around trauma-informed universal approaches. For example, every time I'm in a room I assume that the person or people I'm talking to might have experienced what we're talking about. If I'm in a room full of social workers they might have been in care, they might have been sexually abused, they might have had a parent in prison. So, again it is that whole sense that if we can hold that in mind and it's that whole not us and them. And I guess it is also around, sometimes it is obvious, if someone has had medical trauma, that they might hear a siren from an ambulance, and something might be activating and painful. But as you said often, we don't know, or it has been embedded or held in a somatic memory.

It might be preverbal or in utero. It might be something locked or hidden away. Something we might have dissociated from. And then something might happen at work, and it just unexpectedly catapults us down a time hole or we have a reaction or response but don't know or have a clear narrative or sense of why. But it feels painful, wounding, unnerving, tender. It might just feel not right, or spiky, or we might feel it in our bodies.

And so, if you don't have the psychological safety or trust to name that or say that, or have someone who recognises that, or just realises that this work can be really tough. Or on the other side, are fearful you will be judged, stigmatised, negatively portrayed, viewed as not coping, and so forth. Then where we go with these experiences, and how they might build up and come out or show themselves in other ways. I guess we really need individual, collective, and organisational things to support and buffer our emotional and physical and spiritual and organisational immune systems. And for people, in this work, to be able to be reflective and reflexive about what they bring and what we need—holding in mind that we will all have hotspots and tender points. And these can change or shift at different times and with different people.

Lisa So, moving towards thinking about ancestral trauma. In the section of the book that our conversation is in, the other chapters feature thinking around Islamophobia and anti-racism and allyship. If we're thinking about the impact of ancestral trauma, how would you widen that frame beyond what has already been discussed in this section of the book in our thinking around ancestral trauma?

Karen Another big topic that we won't be able to do justice to but an area I am very passionate about and interested in is ancestral trauma. It has many different definitions and notions but in essence it often refers to the psychological, emotional, physiological, cultural, and spiritual effects, patterns, and responses that can be passed down and through multiple generations. Much like intergenerational trauma, and they are often used interchangeably. But a lot of work on ancestral trauma often, but not exclusively, refers to the collective trauma and shared histories experienced by for example an ethnic, cultural, or familial group due to historical events. Such as the Rwandan genocide, the Troubles, forced displacement, the Holocaust, slavery, famine, war, so many. And how this might shape and influence behaviours, beliefs, ways of being and relating, narratives, responses of people's children and children's children, descendants. Even if they didn't directly experience that trauma. So, for example, unexplained hypervigilance, survivors' guilt, overprotectiveness of one's children, understandable distrust of organisations and institutions, and so forth. There are huge bodies of literature on some of these patterns and possible impacts and one of the future books I hope to write. There is also ancestral hope, wisdom, courage, and all sorts which is important too. So we need the both/and.

It's really interesting because one of my favourite days of my whole training as a clinical psychologist was when we spent two whole days with one person, who we felt comfortable with. I picked one of my best friends on the course, and we did a cultural genogram, we really went into the different layers and textures. I spent most of the two days crying, stuff came up that maybe I hadn't thought about on a deep emotional level. With ancestral trauma, we might say and know certain narratives, but for some of us, there's so much of those hidden stories, the themes of persecution, of migration, of discrimination, and so much more. I had grandparents who were in the Holocaust and then went to apartheid South Africa. My friend had parents from very different countries and backgrounds and also had themes of migration, persecution, othering, and more. Together we started to notice things that have been recreated through different generations; of course, there were other threads of the picture, but it was powerful to think about the different parts of our identity that have been fore-fronted and others which had been less seen or acknowledged. We reflected a lot on how these themes might show themselves or influence our lens, filter, biases, needs, and much more. It is an ongoing journey but such a powerful one. I, probably on a yearly basis, revisit and reflect and add to that genogram. And try to widen and enrich on it.

I think we have a tapestry and a kaleidoscope of our identities, and there are so many different layers and threads, often ever evolving and interconnected. And within this, it is so important that we honour and create space for lots of the different layers. And how they might look and feel differently to different people at different times. Really fits with the importance around cultural humility and reflectivity. All of those aspects including the social GRACES (Burnham and Alison Roper-Hall, 1998),[1] sexuality, gender, language, race, geography, age, ability, appearance, spirituality, religion, ethnicity, relationship status, economic status, class, culture, education, amongst others. And these will also have different relationships to power and privilege. As well as shaped by different levels of identity such as social, cultural, personal, and professional identities. And some of these might be more seen or unseen, or more or less visible, for example, around the colour of one's skin, or if someone is in a wheelchair. And some might be less visible or known, for example, someone might be white but be Jewish, or from the travelling community, or from the Ukraine, and all of the nuances and textures within this. Or we might see someone wearing a hijab but what that means or looks like to that person, and then to others, and then all the other aspects of their other parts of their identity are far more nuanced. Another example might be someone from Syria, who is married to someone from England, and is gay and lives in central London who also has a diagnosis of multiple sclerosis—there are so many layers, and ones which haven't been mentioned or may shift and change, and the important bit is the person's meaning making and sense making.

And with ancestral trauma, some people might know a lot, some people might know very little, some have heard lots, or see the scars, or have names as reminders. Others might have been told very little or have not had the opportunities to have the discussion. For example, people haven't been able to ask their parents or grandparents but have experienced a type of parenting, that they haven't understood the context or where that pattern has come from, because it's been marinated in secrecy, silence, or shame, but yet it has influenced and had a big impact on their here and now. Sometimes, when people or if people find out it can connect the dots or make some sense as to why someone might respond in the way they did.

There is so much in the intergenerational trauma field about communication patterns and also what happens if things are silenced or not spoken about, and we know this can happen on a more collective and community level through societal dissociation or amnesia—whether this is in the erasure or revision of history, the get on it with it, the people not speaking or going back to how things were, the silence, the "forgetting" and much more.

So, it is something that varies on the level of acknowledgement and knowledge it might have. The area of intergenerational, inherited, ancestral trauma is often not in the public sphere in the same way, and lots of clinicians or practitioners are less aware of it. It is often not spoken about and can be neglected or sidelined. Or if it is it is either super science-y like epigenetics led or very psychodynamic, I guess that's why you wanted to shine a light on it in this conversation. And there are so many different aspects within it, from whether looking at it from a genocide perspective, through to slavery, through to the parent-child attachment relationship will be very different and for each person and context.

Lisa Yes. And I wonder why that is. Of course you've raised the issue that we're speaking on a very complex subject, but also I guess there's a deep lack of understanding around the impact of those that came before us, because it's a very westernised, individualised lens, isn't it? This idea that the person in front of you just landed, whereas much more indigenous ways of thinking about who we are, are deeply connected to our ancestral heritage.

Karen Yep, it is so big, and yes, can be very individualised and westernised. And indigenous knowledge and practices can be unfortunately and unfairly positioned as a bit "woo woo" and so can be discounted, othered, or sidelined. In practice, in research, in interventions, and so many other areas. There can certainly be the privileging of western knowledge and othering, shaming, and stigma around. And people, communities, and society can be disconnected from collective and shared histories and experiences, and we know wider aspects such as traditional healing practices, routines, rituals, traditions, local knowledge, embodied wisdom, and so much more. And within this topic it is not just intergenerational trauma, intergenerational wisdom, intergenerational healing, intergenerational connection, and much more.

Lisa Sometimes I do find myself in training raising the impacts of colonisation, slavery, partition, and various other historical and ancestral traumas that were hugely traumatic and traumatising; I can see that for some people they're thinking about that for the first time. So it's a subject we need to tread gently and carefully and thoughtfully.

Karen Hugely. We do need to tread gently and be mindful how it is said or shared but also is so important to be named, and spoken about, and bought into spaces. But I hear you it can be overwhelming. It can make people feel guilt, shame, discomfort, frustration, powerless, attacked, threatened, criticised, blamed, and much more. For some it can feel very very close and personal and for others can feel very disconnected and distanced and not directly applicable to them. For some it fits and makes sense, others it can be so unfamiliar and different territory. It can be so wrapped up in so many layers and levels. Including now lots around the political and cultural contexts around what people have experienced or not experienced, around what people have learned in schools or through the news and their sources of info, around the current polarisation and discourses and responses around "wokeness." It is so layered.

And on a very different level but also important is something like school. Often it is not just how a child is doing or feeling in school, but this is often wrapped up and influenced by the parent or carer's own experience to school. Might also be, for example, around their other children's experience at school. As well as feelings and thoughts about the school system. Might also be historical experiences around school, and so much more. What their learning and education and school experience was like. What messages and discourses did they get marinated in around school and how have these influenced them now? So, these things can consciously or unconsciously shape. For example, when a parent has to go to speak to the head teacher, or they get feedback from a teacher, or their child is being bullied, or they have a letter sent home, or have to go to "parents" evening, or have to support their child with their homework, or told their child is struggling etc.

Lisa You've had experiences working with communities who have experienced and suffered genocide. Is there anything that you have learned that feels relevant for this conversation? That you bring into thinking about how we care for the people who care?

Karen I love that question. There's so many things. Let me think about some of the key things. I've been very privileged to have worked in lots of countries postwar, and genocide, as well as other huge sorts of collective and community traumas. I think some of the key things is around honouring the diversity of impact and response, and how people cope or make sense of what has happened, what their needs are or might be, not lumping people together, and giving people a menu of options, and being led by them. There are lots of different culturally sensitive local practices including some community-led justice and reconciliation methods which I have been honoured to be included in, and I think there is a lot to learn from them—like with most things, mixed, and blended and landed differently for different people. These often have a focus on truth telling, on acknowledgement of harm, of sometimes forgiveness. But also recognise that healing is relational and happens in relationships and in communities and not in isolation. For example, in Rwanda, they had the Gacaca courts, in South Africa, the Truth and Reconciliation Commission, in Uganda, the Mato Oput, in Botswana and some other countries, the Kgotia, and many others. And of course, there are much more local healing practices whether that is around certain rituals, traditions, and healing ceremonies.

> **Gacaca Courts** were based on restorative justice for those who were remorseful for their role during the genocide.[2]
> **Truth and Reconciliation Commission** was set up to help deal with what happened under apartheid.[3]
> **Mato Oput** is a traditional approach to forgiveness and reconciliation specific to the Acholi people, an ethnic group from Northern Uganda. Acholi traditions centre the principles and practices of reconciliation, healing, forgiveness, and amnesty.[4]
> **Kgotia** is a community-led meeting where decisions are arrived at by consensus.[5]

There are a lot of aspects which are focused on trying to repair the social bonds and the sense of community which for many was ruptured and tore. In some countries or places within these countries this is things like shared building projects or repairing of infrastructure. For others, it is creating shared murals or symbols. For others, it might be around human libraries or through theatre.

There is also so much around the impact of hurt and suffering and pain and the many intergenerational layers. For example, in Rwanda, the number of children born from rape, people widowed or children orphaned, houses or communities destroyed, the amount of people who contracted HIV, the loss of the financial support to the household due to often death or the person being imprisoned–the ripples and layers go on a long time after the event. Including how parents or grandparents talk or tell their children about what happened or understand why they might parent the way they do and so much more.

On a different note, but so important, I think the inclusion of the body is beyond important whether that is around drumming circles, rhythm, chanting, dancing, shaking it off, music, singing, poetry, choirs, orchestras, or collective circles of spirituality and faith. For lots of different people creative expression through storytelling, art, and the power of community, having those spaces of solidarity, having cultural affinity groups, or healing circles is where people are able to come together and have opportunities for joy and lightness. They also can be spaces for unity and collective healing. They also can create opportunities for movement which can be so important in the context of trauma, including stuckness, powerlessness, feeling trapped, and so much more.

I also learned a lot not just in Rwanda but in much of my time in Africa around the role of faith, as well as the connection and role to nature. And without having some of the systems, organisations, and processes which we have—the power of the community and people and communities resourcing, creativity, and survivorship. And throughout my work with trauma, the importance of honouring, enriching, and respecting the healing, wisdom, and strengths that people, communities, families, and systems can have.

I will stop there, but the richness is hard to put into words

Lisa   I really wanted to highlight intergenerational trauma and your experiences of genocide to bring two incredibly large subjects into the book to spark an interest for people who might not have worked in this area, to learn more. I also really wanted to add that when we're caring for people in organisations, if we work from a trauma-informed basis, we have the best chance of not adding to harm. Part of that trauma-informed way of working and viewing the world and the people within it gifts us with an opportunity to be thoughtful, curious, and reflective about not just thinking around policies but rather broadening the way we think about people by considering subjects as large as intergenerational trauma. We cannot know what we have not lived . . .

Reflection

Bringing such a huge and complex area into one chapter in this book was a challenge but Karen has managed to bring so much for the reader to consider. It didn't start with me. Or you. There are parts of us that we may never understand as we carry within our bodies all that went before us. Thinking in this way invites a very different approach to how we care for each other.

Discussion Points

1. **Understanding Intergenerational Trauma**
   - How might trauma experienced by previous generations shape the behaviours and responses of individuals and families today?
   - In what ways do I recognise the influence of familial patterns (e.g., care experience, incarceration, substance abuse) in my work with others or within myself?

2. **Recognising Ancestral Trauma**
    - How does the legacy of historical events like slavery, colonisation, or forced displacement continue to impact people today?
    - What steps can I take to better understand and respond to the effects of ancestral trauma in the communities I serve?
3. **Importance of Supervision and Reflective Practice**
    - How do my current supervisory and reflective practices support the well-being of staff who may have experienced trauma?
    - What policies or processes in my organisation help ensure a trauma-informed and psychologically safe working environment?
4. **Trauma-Informed Approaches**
    - Do I assume that colleagues or service users may be carrying unseen trauma in my interactions with them?
    - How can I embed trauma-informed principles more deeply into my everyday practice?
5. **Widening the Frame of Ancestral Trauma**
    - How might ancestral trauma show up differently across diverse cultural or historical backgrounds?
    - Am I broadening my understanding of trauma to include collective, historical, and systemic dimensions?
6. **Integrating Intergenerational Wisdom and Healing**
    - In what ways can I acknowledge and value the cultural strengths and wisdom passed down through generations?
    - How do I create space in my practice for cultural heritage, traditions, or languages that promote healing and resilience?
7. **Complexity and Societal Dissociation**
    - Do I feel discomfort or resistance when engaging with painful aspects of collective history?

- How can I approach discussions of trauma and historical injustice with more empathy and understanding?
8. **Integrating Healing and Reconnection**
    - How can I honour and integrate intergenerational strengths, traditions, and cultural practices in my work or personal healing?
    - In what ways can reconnecting with ancestral knowledge and cultural identity support collective and personal well-being?

Notes

1 The term social GGRRAAACCEEESSS is an acronym that describes aspects of personal and social identity which afford people different levels of power and privilege: Gender Geography Race Religion Age Ability Appearance Culture Class/caste Education Employment Ethnicity Spirituality Sexuality Sexual orientation. It was developed and designed by John Burnham and Alison Roper-Hall (1993, 1998).
2 https://www.un.org/en/preventgenocide/rwanda/assets/pdf/Backgrounder%20Justice%202014.pdf.
3 https://www.apartheidmuseum.org/exhibitions/the-truth-and-reconciliation-commission-trc.
4 https://www.gendersecurityproject.com/decolonial-healing-justice/mato-oput.
5 https://www.tageo.com/index-e-sf-v-09-d-m1815952.htm.

Reference

Burnham, J. (2013). Developments in social GGRRAAACCEEESSS: Visible, invisible, voiced–unvoiced. In Krause, I. (ed.) *Culture and Reflexivity in Systemic Psychotherapy: Mutual Perspectives*. London: Karnac.

PART THREE
Pledge

11
Introduction to Part Three

There have so far been many ideas, road maps, and suggestions for how to take forward caring for the people who care within this book. But in this section, I wanted to call it "Pledge" because my hope is that you will be moved to action; it will ask you to consider what you will pledge that you will do differently, either individually or systemically.

Feeling cared for and from a place of knowledge that if we're working alongside trauma, then it is part of the work that it will impact us in some way, is more than just ticking that box. Fully understanding that we are working alongside trauma means that we have intentional ways of doing things that truly sit in the heart of trauma-informed practice.

Reflecting on the contents of the book so far, here are some prompts that can be used as journal reflections, supervision discussion points, or in-team development sessions. They are deep questions and need to be held carefully and sensitively in group discussions.

1. What does caring for myself feel like?
2. What does feeling cared for by an organisation look like?

3. What does belonging mean to you, personally and professionally?
4. What does mattering mean to you, personally and professionally?
5. How does your team create a sense of belonging for all members, especially those from marginalised backgrounds?
6. Reflect on a recent situation where your care felt honoured or overlooked. What did you learn?
7. What is one micro-action you can take this week to promote care for yourself or for others in your role?
8. How would a new staff member know that the organisation you work in has staff well-being embedded, not just on paper, but in practice?

When done well, there is an acknowledgement and understanding that we're on a learning journey. Striking the balance changes and is reflected upon regularly. Ultimately, we're seeking to create a foundation of psychological safety.

Enjoy this final section, gaining more insights, as Sophie talks about how her own lived experiences of adversity have impacted how she leads in her school and connects with others who share lived experiences of adversity. I then talk with Lou who shares about her own journey to becoming a trauma therapist and how that model works in the addiction space. Amelia and I explore menopause from a strengths-based perspective rather than a medical one, and the section ends with Lisa Lea Weston on the vital component to any trauma-informed practice journey: supervision.

12

A Conversation With Sophie Tales

Harnessing Educators' Lived Experiences of Adversity

Opening this section, Sophie's call to action is on how we understand the lived experiences of our team and the impact that they may or may not have on the work. This exploration is rich in considerations of doing our own work in order that we may meet children and young people more deeply.

Lisa   What do you do in your work and what sort of role do you have?

Sophie   I am the Vice Principal (Deputy Head Teacher) of a two form entry mainstream primary school in Leicester City.

Lisa   Have you always been in teaching?

Sophie   Yes. After I graduated, I completed a year as a manager of a tuition centre, and decided that teaching was what I wanted to do, so I completed a PGCE (Postgraduate Certificate in Education).

Lisa You're the author of a book that explores those who work in schools and are also recovering from childhood adversity or have recovered from childhood adversity (Tales, 2024). I was fortunate enough to write the foreword for that book because, of course, it's a huge interest of mine in terms of thinking about trauma-informed settings, services, and systems. Largely because if we don't take care of our staff, then how on earth are we going to take care of anyone else? So tell me a bit about how you came to write that book. What came up for you that made you feel so compelled by the subject that you had to write a book about it?

Sophie I think the origins of the book (Tales, 2024), if I really look back and think about it, stem from working at a special school that specialised in social, emotional, mental health (SEMH) and it was a school that really championed relationships. A school that you could only really have success in by connecting with pupils and when I say success, I mean success in supporting the students, helping them to regulate or helping them reach their goals—whether that be academic or vocational qualifications.

You could only support that success if you were willing and able to really share yourself and share yourself in its entirety, be very transparent and open about where you were in your lived experience, and the lessons you'd learnt along the way. I loved working at that school. I have wonderful memories of working at that school.

It was quite obvious, or rather it felt really obvious to me, that the staff who had the most success were the staff who knew themselves, whether that's because they'd been to therapy or had a stable understanding of self or they were older so had more lived experience to draw upon.

The staff who didn't have success, it sometimes felt that they were almost being coached alongside the kids in becoming self-aware. And it was on this realisation that I realised that I had taken for granted how well I knew myself and the skills I had learnt through my own adversity. I'd taken it for granted my ability to be able to connect with people very quickly and that that in itself was a response from living through trauma.

My ability to connect with people quickly is a way of providing safety for myself—whether that's emotional or physical safety. If I connect with you quickly, if I build a relationship with you quickly, you are less likely to emotionally hurt me and I can judge how to protect myself from you. But it's also because I get a real thrill out of connecting with people. I find people fascinating—again I think that's because I've done so much work on myself I am interested in the psychology of others and what makes others tick—to learn about that you have to connect with someone—so I almost speed up the process.

Lisa I love that you've raised that particular skill which you've considered as a result of your experiences of adversity and trauma response, as we met a few years ago at a conference that I was speaking at. The first thing that you said to me was "my name's Sophie and you're going to be my new best friend." I thought this was hilarious and we've been friends ever since!

When you're describing that as a response to your experiences to ensure quick and safe connection, providing emotional stability, I think that's really insightful and nuanced and helps us think about the children and young people that we work with.

Sophie Yes definitely. I think I can read people very quickly. I have a skill in that area. I could see those skills in other people and I was a bit fed up of the narrative of if you've been through abuse, these are the difficulties you have to go through. If you've been through trauma, this is the shit you've got to slog through. And I thought actually, a lot of my best skills come from trauma.

I would say a lot of my really fine-tuned skills are from trauma and I was fed up of that negative narrative around that. And when I looked at colleagues who were incredible with these children who were going through so much, they were amazing at it because they themselves had either been through similar experiences and learned from it.

And that's the key bit; it's not that they've been through experiences full stop. It's more like . . . They're a wizard at connecting with people, they've been through experiences, learned about themselves and *now* they're a wizard at connecting with people. And I thought how can I capture that? How can I also tap into this unspoken thing that we seem to have in the education sector where we don't talk about educators as human beings, we talk about them as robots?

And how can I write something that will support cracking open personality and leading humanly with students that you work with? But in a way that supports staff in still feeling safe as professionals, because we need to have those boundaries there, that's equally important. But I just think you get the best out of kids if you're able to give a bit of yourself too.

So yeah that's where it came from, in as much of a nutshell as I can do.

Lisa From writing about this and your discussions with those who work in education having recovered from adversity and/or trauma, what has been your greatest learning around how we care for those who care and what they need?

Sophie The first thing that comes to my head is allowing space for the person you are supporting to tell you what they feel they need. Not assuming to know the solution to what they are going through because you are their manager.

In senior leadership within a school you're not just holding the experiences of children, you're holding the historic and present experiences of staff. You may have members of staff who are cancer survivors, are still fighting cancer, who have loved ones who have dementia—just as a few examples!

So you're attempting to help a community thrive whilst supporting individuals through some of their hardest life experiences—adults and children alike.

So to not listen to what an individual person is saying that they need through their very specific set of circumstances is to ignore the self-awareness that individual may well have. Personally I have had amazing line managers and I've had really poor line managers. My poorest line managers have been line managers that I've gone to with an experience I am going through and said I think this is what I need and they have completely ignored my own perspective of what I feel I need to be able to support myself to continue to work or to continue to manage within the role. As a manager, you can't always grant every request—however the conversation needs to start with the request and then consider what you are feasibly able to manage as a school.

Lisa How do you think people in leadership can manage that tension of, as you've said, meeting the needs of the children and young people, the core anchor of our work, while also at the same time being able to meet the needs of the staff team? Do you feel that there's a tension sometimes between those two things and how do you manage that?

Sophie Oh, completely, definitely a tension because you want to support everyone equally all the time. The reality is that's not always possible. It doesn't mean that we don't strive for it but dealing with what we're dealing with in the education sector and the public sector as a whole, you're not going to be able to manage supporting everyone perfectly all the time.

I find the best way of aiming to support everyone against the restraints we have is by being aware of what support I have on offer and in my toolbox at any given time. So I consider it in the same way that I do my own self-care toolbox. I've got my box of stuff that's working for me at the minute to help me feel regulated and calm at the end of a workday.

Whether that's that a particular podcast is working for me at the minute or going for a walk with the dog is working for me at the minute. I've got my box in my head of strategies and tools that I can go to if I feel dysregulated. In my book (Tales, 2024) I provide strategies for educators on how to support children in creating their own tool box of self-regulating strategies that can help in the classroom—so that tool box works for adults or children—it's individual to what you need at the time.

I also know what is in my tool box for what support I'm able to give to staff. Whether that's when I'm navigating the diary for a particular week, I see that there's a little bit of flex in cover support—so I know that I've got X periods available during a working week that I could give to somebody if they come to me in crisis and say, I need some space, right? I know I've got that to offer. So I think almost having an ongoing audit really of what support you have on offer to be able to give and I think being really transparent with that as well is really important.

Lisa You've mentioned your own tool kit and also how that works for you personally. In doing so you also share what the tool kit is that you have at school to offer others. Somewhere within that of course is perhaps supporting people in how to develop their own tool kit. You mentioned earlier that sometimes there might be an age differential that makes a difference.

So how do you support your staff in terms of developing their social, emotional mental health and well-being? And is that the role of the leadership team in a school or in any organisation?

Sophie I think that is something that's really at the front of my mind at the minute—is what is our threshold? What is school's threshold? It's something I'm constantly having to think about at the moment because it feels like, weekly, at the minute, there is something else that schools are taking on. I try and make this a part of any conversation that I'm having with anyone who is either working inside schools or outside of schools because I think it's really important to talk about.

Within the last year, schools are now doing their own early help offer. So, the lowest band of social care is now undertaken by teachers who are now doing their own social care intervention. So what used to be completely dealt with by social care is now dealt with by schools. So that is now part of school's threshold. We are now holding the mental health in schools team (MHST), which is a band below the Child and Adolescent Mental Health Team (CAMHS) because CAMHS is so stretched. So that's part of schools' threshold. In terms of attendance and making sure that children are going into school, the educational welfare team, which used to be provided to school as part of the local authority statutory offer, now has to be paid for by school or the work, is completed internally within school. So that's now a part of school's threshold.

In terms of health care, there used to be a school nurse in every school—that is no more. I can send off a referral to a school nurse and if it meets thresholds, they will come into school; if not, the parent has to fight to get a GP appointment.

We are no longer education institutions. We are first response, on the ground response units to any kind of need, whether that's child or parent. So when it comes then to staff and helping them to become more aware of themselves and their own mental health. Do I think it's right that it's part of school's threshold? No. Do I think that it's necessary to make sure that people are safe and well? Yes. Because unfortunately there's a lot of things we're now doing to make sure that society is safe and well. Yeah. I do take that on underneath my umbrella of responsibilities because there's a little bit of me that goes if we don't, who will?

Lisa And I think you're right. I think lots of people outside of an education setting would be unaware of that. I've always felt that schools should do all of that. I believe that should be in the context of the correct funding and resources being made available in order to do so. Should school be expected to do this while not having any new funding and particular types of staff within a school? No. However I do think that schools make the best settings for community care of children, young people, and families. It's interesting because all of the things that you're talking about are one of the reasons why for me supervision is essential, but is supervision seen as a priority? That's another question and one explored in my chapter with Lisa Lea Weston in Chapter 12.

Understanding the context as you laid it out, what are the implications then for staff with trauma and adversity histories that are unhealed or not being worked on, what are the implications then for the community using the school?

Sophie I think we are doing so much more and I agree with you. Part of the reason why I loved working in a special school was because it was so holistic because it absolutely had to be and I do agree that schools have the perfect structure to be able to be that community hub but exactly like you say, we also need the money and the staff and the training to be able to do it well without causing damage and a lot of the time, that's where I go back to is damage limitation—is this safely within my school's threshold?

I'm in charge of safeguarding. I will have parents that come in who for instance I might have a mum come in and show me a wound that their partner was subjecting on them the night before, and I'm the first person that they've spoken to about it.

I have to very carefully consider within that conversation what I am skilled in to be able to support that parent with without causing further damage. I am not a trained counsellor, but I am an empathetic, trained, known person within the community that can listen and can care and can provide space.

I'm also educated and connected enough within our school unit to be able to say the other services that parent can then connect with and signpost and, so in the same instance, I think, with staff, I am not a therapist, but I am a known person, a supportive figure, someone they know, a familiar person, who can provide space, who can listen and, again, can signpost on and know what's in the tool box. Examples might be communication with external agencies to the school, signposting support and typical structures within a school that can be adapted to best support the school's community. Awareness of what's on offer in the area of a school is pivotal to best support those who are most in need.

Lisa Within that, while you're speaking, I can feel the potential for the pressure upon one person, in this instance, you.

Sophie It's huge. I can feel it in my body while I'm talking to you. It's weighty. It's weighty because it's incredibly important work. However, it's also so important that those doing the important work are being provided with the supervision they need to keep doing this important work. As the threshold for schools increases, how are we ensuring that our staff are being looked after?

Lisa What were your key findings in your book? What were the key findings around caring for those who care, who also have trauma and adversity histories?

Sophie I think that overall, the main theme was around allowing individuality. Increasingly we're seeing, particularly in secondary schools, quite a uniformed approach towards behaviour, a uniformed approach towards teaching and learning and almost scripted ways of teaching, which I'm not opposed to wholeheartedly. There are parts of both of those structures that can be used very effectively— as long as they are providing the opportunity for nuance and flex and individuality. I think that was a massive part of the interviews that I had with people within my book, was they needed to have the agency to be able to be themselves, to be able to connect as their authentic self.

Another key finding was for there to be an understanding that everyone is very much going through a journey, that none of us are a finished article. And I think that particularly more so for those of us who have been through trauma or those of us who have been through adversity, that it never ends. The things you learn about yourself or the parts of your childhood that might pop up when you really weren't expecting them, you'd therapised every section and last corner of it, you didn't think you needed to return to it. So I think, the overwhelming feeling from having spoken to people and interviewed people for the book was for managers and staff around them to just hold space. I've certainly found that in different schools that I've worked in and different roles that I've worked in, I've needed space in different ways and support in different ways. The best way to get the most out of me, so from a business model, if you want to get your value for money out of me, then you need to hear me and listen to me. If I'm going through an experience, support me in whatever way feels best. Because once I've bounced back, I bounce back hard and will graft because I, and as others in the book stated, I have a vested interest that doesn't come from wanting to earn a particular wage or anything really like that.

If you are from adversity and your values align to being an educator because you so desperately want to be the person you didn't have, well as an employer, you've then got someone who is going to grind and work to the bone because they have an intrinsic motivation to do so that is nothing to do with anything that you have to give other than supporting them in continuing to work. The educators that I interviewed for my book all spoke of their unique experiences and how their individuality helps them support others going through similar experiences.

Lisa I think that's an absolutely beautiful acknowledgement, recognition, insight, and understanding that means that when we are working alongside people who are motivated by the normal things that people get motivated by, which is money, being approved of, having an important-sounding job title, then we know it. We know when we are working with those people, because when we work with people, as you so beautifully said, then you have people in your workforce who are giving you their soul. I often say if I was a lady that lunched, I would still be doing this.

Reflection

This conversation really supported thinking about the impact of our own experiences upon the work that we do, what we bring with us that is known to us but also that which is not known to us. An important part of the discussion to note is when Sophie talks about what is happening in her body as she considers the experience of the pressure felt in the role that she has in her school. Sophie is talking about the language of the central nervous system and how it reacts to the world, leading us straight back to considering polyvagal theory mentioned earlier in the book and also in Amelia's chapter in this section.

Discussion Points

1. **Self-Awareness and Emotional Intelligence**
   - How has my own self-awareness or emotional growth impacted the way I support students or colleagues?
   - In what ways do I continue to develop self-awareness in my role?

2. **Valuing Lived Experience in Education**
   - How do I recognise and utilise the lived experiences of staff as assets in our work with students?
   - Have I created safe spaces for staff to reflect on and learn from their past adversity or trauma? And in what ways does my own life experience enhance or limit my empathy and connection with others?

3. **Compassionate and Boundaried Leadership**
   - How do I strike the balance between being compassionate and maintaining professional boundaries as a leader?
   - Are there situations where I've struggled to balance empathy with maintaining clear roles or expectations?

4. **Building and Maintaining a Tool Box of Support**
   - What specific support tools and resources do I currently offer to staff, and how often are these reviewed?
   - How transparent am I with my team about what support is available and what isn't—and do staff know where and how to access different kinds of support when they need it?

5. **The Changing Role of Schools**
   - In what ways has my role (or the role of our school) shifted beyond education to include social care and mental health support?
   - What training or resources do I or my team need to safely meet these expanding responsibilities?

6. **Supervision and Reflective Practice**
   - How often do I engage in or provide supervision, and how meaningful is it in supporting staff well-being?
   - How could our reflective spaces be improved to better meet the emotional and professional needs of our team?

7. **Individuality and Authenticity in Practice**
   - How do I support staff in bringing their authentic selves to work while maintaining consistent practice and professionalism?
   - In what ways can we balance structured policies with flexibility that honours personal connection?
8. **Listening, Motivation, and Growth**
   - What systems are in place to ensure staff feel heard, empowered, and supported in their personal and professional growth?
   - Am I fostering a culture where ongoing development and agency are seen as essential parts of workplace well-being?

Reference

Tales, S. (2024). *Creating Adversity-Aware Schools: Trauma-Informed Tools and Strategies from Educators with Lived Experience*. Jessica Kingsley Publishers.

13
A Conversation With Lou Lebentz
Lessons From Psychotherapy About Trauma

The helping professions attract many who have walked through the fires of their own personal challenges, whether knowingly or unknowingly at the outset. This chapter explores the intertwining of personal experiences, trauma, and professional journeys, examining how they shape not only our paths into the field but also our capacity to hold space for others. It also shines a light on the critical role of self-awareness, healing, and understanding in developing authentic, trauma-informed practitioners. Through this lens, we uncover the depths of the work and its transformative potential—not just for those we serve, but for ourselves.

Lisa What led you into the helping profession? And did you begin your career in the trauma field or elsewhere?

Lou What led me into the helping profession, in hindsight, was probably my own trauma and my own family of origin material. I didn't begin my career in the helping profession. I started working firstly in the fashion industry and

	rag trade and then I moved into radio and finally into rehab, working in one. So, I started in the addiction field to begin with and not trauma.
Lisa	It's interesting that we separate out addiction and trauma in traditional thinking yet addiction, we would argue, is a manifestation of unhealed trauma.
Lou	This separation between trauma and addiction in traditional thinking is one of the core challenges we face today, and this urgently needs to change. By integrating trauma into the addiction narrative, we allow for a fuller, more compassionate understanding of the roots of addictive behaviours, paving the way for far deeper healing and recovery.
Lisa	You're a psychotherapist now . . .
Lou	I am a psychotherapist, although my journey to becoming one was a long one. It began with training in neurolinguistic programming (NLP) and clinical hypnosis in my early 30s. I'd left the fashion industry at 24 after being sectioned with psychosis. That marked my first awakening, if you like, and sparked my interest in psychology and mental health. I dabbled with therapy, but not deeply, and started reading books like *A Layman's Guide to Psychiatry and Psychoanalysis* (Berne, 1971). Yet, I still wasn't ready to become a therapist. Instead, I went into radio and carried on my old ways of drinking, smoking, and partying, avoiding my trauma and mental health distress. In my early 30s, my mother called me while she was up a mountain in Italy with my stepfather. I had gone to help get him into treatment for alcoholism—a journey that took two years. Nursing him and witnessing their divorce made me question my own addictions and reawakened

my interest in my earlier mental health challenges. When I returned to the UK, I pursued NLP and clinical hypnotherapy training but quickly realised these modalities weren't enough for me. My passion in addiction drove me to complete a six-month full-time addiction therapy course at the Priory Hospital in Bristol. That led to my first job, at about 35 or 36, in an addiction treatment unit at the Priory Roehampton.

During my eight years at the Priory, I finally began to recognise my own trauma. I'd go home in tears, triggered by the horrendous life stories I heard. It was here I realised my issues extended beyond addiction and codependency. I had an awful lot of unresolved trauma that needed addressing.

Lisa In your work now, you're in the position where you lead and look after a lot of other psychotherapists and counsellors. In your experience, is it very usual that people come into the profession and *then* discover that they have trauma or do you think that people experience trauma and then choose to come into the profession? In other words, do you think the profession triggers a deeper understanding in a person or do you think that the understanding is there and that's what brings people into the profession?

Lou I think it's both. It can be either or, but I think that anybody who is in this profession that doesn't think in part that they are being drawn into this profession because of their own personal experiences needs a bit of a wake-up call. "Healer heal thyself" is the phrase and we are often led into this work because we need to do the work. Being in this profession must lead us to doing our own work because otherwise you can't functionally sustain it as a career; some clinicians keep doing it perhaps, but they must be doing it from a dissociated position which isn't helpful for anyone. But I also think you can't really understand how to sit with other people's deeper feelings and distress unless you've done your own work or at least started. We need to be able to swim into the depths of the ocean of our own somatic system and body before we can be great at helping or holding other people to do the same. It takes practice and a lot of work on us and yet I always joke with people that, if I could go back 22 years to the people that I was first a therapist with, I'd give them their money back. Because there is no way my ability to contain and stay with people's emotions and distress was anywhere near the level or capacity I can manage today.

Lisa I can't quite remember whether I said this or someone else did, but I always say, we can only meet someone as deeply as we've met ourselves.

Lou Yes, so I use a nautical metaphor for everything because I run a program called The Voyage®. So, to reiterate, I always say to clinicians, coaches, therapists, and mental health practitioners that we have to get people back into the ocean and swimming in the sea. Because the sea is their own body and their own somatic system, and we can only lead somebody down into the depths of their own somatic system to the level that we have travelled ourselves. If we haven't travelled into the deep, dirty, misty waters and we're scared of the sea, all we're going to do is bring that person back up. We will unconsciously even be communicating that we don't want them to "go there" so we keep quite surface level and surface structured. But what that person needs and also probably wants is more of a dolphin swimming alongside them, somebody who has the skills to stay deep with them and can shine a torchlight down into the darker waters and keep going. That way they will be communicating it's okay, I'm with you and I can stay with you, and you can cope with this. You've got this and I've got you too.

Lisa Having been led into the trauma field through your own awakening, what happened once you understood fully what trauma meant and where did that take you?

Lou Well, I didn't understand fully what trauma meant. I wasn't even aware of trauma until I'd been a therapist, as I said, for four or five years; there was nothing about it in my training. I went on to do a four-year advanced diploma in psychotherapy and I think they had a day or a weekend on trauma. But none of the therapy training came through what I call a trauma lens. It was all outside of a trauma lens and trauma wasn't even mentioned. And I've also got to say that I have clients now who are training as psychotherapists and clinicians, and they are still not being taught through a trauma lens which is quite disturbing.

Lisa Bearing in mind you're working in the field of psychotherapy, for there not to be a trauma lens in that space, it's quite alarming and highlights how difficult it is for people who want to recover through talking therapies to find somebody who actually understands trauma.

Lou The lack of trauma-trained practitioners is indeed alarming, especially given how widespread trauma is and its foundational role in many mental health struggles. Without a trauma lens, practitioners risk misunderstanding their clients' behaviours and symptoms, often pathologising them or seeing them as personal flaws rather than adaptive responses to trauma.

This can lead to interventions that are invalidating, re-traumatising, or simply ineffective. For instance, practitioners may bypass the body entirely, failing to address somatic dysregulation or the ways trauma lives in the nervous system. They may also focus on cognitive approaches without recognising that a dysregulated state makes insight alone insufficient for healing.

It's partly why I wrote The Voyage® because it addresses this gap by equipping practitioners with a deep understanding of trauma through a structured, phased approach. It integrates psychoeducation, somatic work, and an exploration of the mind-body connection, helping therapists to see their clients holistically. Practitioners learn to hold a safe, regulated space, meeting clients where they are and helping them process their experiences at a pace that honours their capacity. This not only fosters deeper healing but also ensures that care is delivered in a way that is both compassionate and profoundly effective. It's also coming from the frame of "what happened to you" rather than "what is wrong with you" which is a new paradigm and much more integrated way of viewing mental health and trauma.

Lisa And that's because most models, if not all models, locate the problem in the person, belonging to the person, almost blaming the person. A trauma lens shifts the whole way that distress is viewed.

Lou Exactly. It was like an epiphany and light bulb moments came one after the other when I did realise and thankfully, I started reading around it even more and discovering all the different aspects of trauma. I started to recognise that there is huge resistance to the word *trauma*, particularly in the addiction field, and among other areas of the profession too.

I think many people feel the term *trauma* is overused yet in my experience, it's actually *underused,* and its definition is way too narrow. Whereas a lot of sceptics now think the definition of it is too wide and invalidates "real" traumatic experience.

Lisa Speaking as somebody who spent some time in a 12-step programme in my early 20s, I've not had a drink since 1990, and I haven't been to a meeting probably since 1995, do you think that the resistance is because in the 12-step model there is a real importance placed on the idea that if we think about trauma, then we're shifting the blame? That we're not taking responsibility, and that we want to blame someone else. For me, exploring trauma was one of the reasons that I stopped going to meetings because I knew I needed to do that next and that space was not the right place for that.

Is it that if we talk about addiction as a trauma response, a self-medication, that somehow some people think that that's using trauma as an excuse, and that that may hamper the recovery journey? Whereas in fact, the opposite is true. In my experience, once there's an understanding, that it's a trauma response, that it's self-medication, then the shame can vanish, the movement forward can appear, and the journey of healing can begin.

Lou I agree, and I am totally with you, and that is absolutely what I believe and what I teach. I think there is resistance for many reasons, your suggestion being a big part of it. I think the other resistance that I come across is that the disease model is so entrenched and so is the 12-step model that it's hard for those devotees to be open to anything else. Also, the old way of dealing with addiction was to always work with the addiction first and then look at the trauma afterwards and that thinking is so entrenched so that a lot of clinicians or treatment centres don't want to mention the trauma or bring up the trauma because they feel it's too much and too soon.

I also think that if it's believed that the addiction is the primary issue, then an addiction can more easily be put down or stopped or controlled. To some degree addiction just being a slice of the pie means that it's more manageable. But if someone thinks that they've got to deal with whatever sits underneath the addiction, for some people, some of the time, that might feel like it's too much, too scary, and too frightening to even comprehend, especially at the beginning of their journey.

Hence, I think there's a reticence. I was just going to say also with trauma, I think that when we start talking about the different aspects of trauma, a lot of people have a problem with some of those aspects. Many people don't realise or understand that trauma is not just big one-off events but that sometimes it's down to something that happened to them or around them in early childhood and in their development, of their brain, their nervous system, and the way they understood themselves in the world. Many people don't want to look at this or to seem like they are blaming their family of origin, so there's a reticence to include anybody else or their history in any way.

Even though we're not blaming parents, and we resist ever explaining it like that because quite honestly parents are doing the hardest job in the world already. A lot of people are under stress, and many are dysregulated; the world can be stressful and if they've had their own trauma that they're unaware of too it adds to the mix. But sometimes people don't want to go there because of how it might impact the way they view their upbringing.

Lisa And that therein lies a lack of understanding about trauma. Not all trauma that happens is someone's fault and in some ways the ACE study (Felitti et al., 1998) has contributed to the idea that all trauma is developmental trauma, and that parents/carers have deliberately caused harm, rather than thinking about the traumas that we can experience that are unavoidable like loss, bereavement, or poor mental health or, you know, any of those aspects, particularly through childhood.

Lou Mark Brayne, a very well-known UK eye movement desensitisation and reprocessing (EMDR) trainer, labels aspects of trauma really well, in that he suggests that people have four aspects of trauma. Firstly, there is an obvious **trauma, Aspect One**, which most people would think about as being traumatic such as a tsunami, or rape, abuse, domestic violence, or war; we used to call it in the old days, "big T" trauma; we don't use that terminology anymore.

An Aspect Two Trauma, which is far less understood, suggests that from the moment we are in utero and throughout infancy, childhood, and even into our teenage years, we rely on a co-regulating caregiver because, as babies and young children, we do not yet have the capacity to regulate ourselves. We need a safe, attuned presence—someone who can act as a scaffold for our nervous system, providing a sense of security that becomes embedded in our bodies and minds. This regulation is not just about physical safety; it is about emotional safety too. We need a caregiver who looks into our eyes lovingly, mirrors our emotions, attunes to our needs, and makes us feel as though we matter.

However, when our primary caregivers have unresolved trauma of their own—whether they are emotionally dysregulated, self-medicating, highly stressed, neglectful, or simply unavailable—this co-regulation does not happen as it should. Instead, we experience a fundamental lack of safety, missing the crucial early experiences of co-regulation and soothing that are essential for our developing nervous system, brain, and overall sense of self.

Beyond this, there is **Aspect Three Trauma**, which occurs when we unconsciously absorb our parents' unresolved trauma and fears. If a parent is deeply fearful—of the sea, wasps, social situations, or any number of things—we often inherit those fears without consciously understanding why.

Then there is **Aspect Four Trauma**, which includes intergenerational and systemic influences—the environment or "soup" in which we grow up. This includes not only our family history but also the broader societal factors that shape our experience: Was there racism, sexism, classism, or homophobia around us? Did we grow up in poverty, an unsafe neighborhood, or even a war zone? What were our schooling experiences like? Were our teachers nurturing or punitive? Did we have safe and supportive friendships?

All of these factors—both personal and societal—play a profound role in shaping our nervous system and the way we understand safety, connection, and belonging in the world.

Lisa It's worth making explicit that we have lots of people in psychotherapy training, people who've undergone training who have no knowledge around trauma and the system and those kind of experiences and who may also be coming to terms with their own life experiences that led them into this work. What's your role and how are you shaping your role in terms of taking some leadership in caring and supporting for those people?

A Conversation With Lou Lebentz

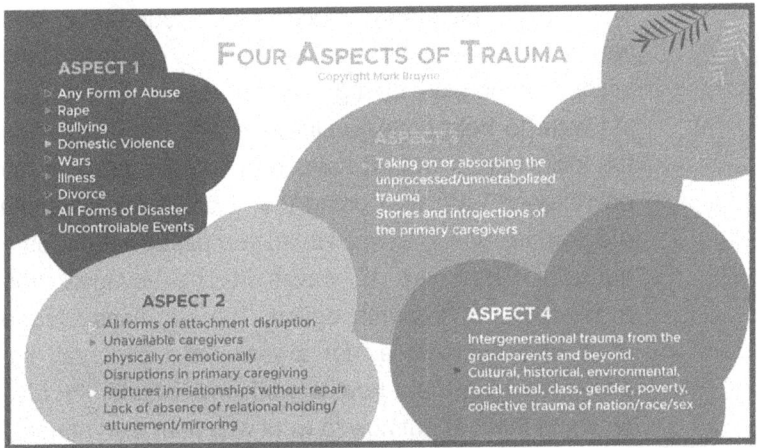

Figure 13.1 The Four Aspects of Trauma

Lou That's a big question and I think that awareness is vital because without awareness, psychoeducation, and being cognisant of what's going on within our own system, we can't move onto the next stage. Hence, I think the first phase is helping people understand by expanding their mind, so they become aware of what trauma is, and its impact, because without understanding that, like I didn't initially, many in the field don't recognise they have anything they need to work on. They might be getting activated frequently in the beginning and return home crying every day like I did but are not sure as to why.

I think we also need to work with the caregiver part of the clinician and ascertain whether in their family of origin did they caretake others and if so, when did it become their role to look after other people and what is that about? Sometimes clinicians and carers need to manage that over-responsibility dynamic they carry for other people because if they don't, they take on too much ownership for the therapeutic outcome and they can also often people please too much or lack boundaries. This was a lot of my early work on my own codependency which I had to work through and process.

I want to help educate clinicians and help them find the skills I know I didn't have in the earlier years of my own career. I am now doing that through my Voyage® programme, which is why I'm such a passionate trauma educator. There are 12 waves in The Voyage® and a 12-week or 12-month option. The clinicians on the deep dive are enrolled for a year, yet I can't say I'm solely teaching them how to work with clients; I'm also teaching them about how to work with their own material and healing. This is because our own personal healing journey is paramount; the more that we can stay with our own distress, discomfort, dysregulation, and start to regulate our system, the better tuning fork or scaffold we are going to be for others, whether that's our clients, our employees, our team; we are going to be that safe other and that's really what we need. We need safety from therapists, coaches, leaders. We need safe others in positions within organisations, the public sector, and in government roles too.

We need more effective leaders who are not going to fall into their younger, more traumatised parts of themselves with the people around them. Rather they're able to stay embodied, regulated, consistent, calm, communicative, compassionate, and all those wonderful aspects and qualities our adult selves do possess when the other younger parts are not being activated.

Lisa   Where are you now in your own healing journey?

Lou   Well, a lot better than where I was 20 years ago thankfully or even 10 years. Yet still on the journey, continuously stepping into the more fully, empowered, authentic,

A Conversation With Lou Lebentz

adult version of myself. I am recognising over time there are far less adapted and wounded parts being activated which means my adult is predominantly the driver of the bus. I always think about people as parts. In trauma therapy we always use a parts model with clients and teach it to them as well. A parts model means we've all got a core adult self, our present moment self who is our "I" self; when a client uses the pronoun "I", it is their adult present moment self who is compassionate, clear, communicative, etc. However, people are not always in their adult "I" selves; multiple times a day they can get triggered out of their adult self into their younger more adapted or wounded parts.

A parts model assists massively because it separates out who the authentic adult self is from the traumatised historical parts who in some way, shape, or form have experienced pain. The younger parts which are made up of the wounded and the adapted were created growing up. Everyone has got some wounding in their younger parts. I just don't think we can get through life without being wounded on some level. The wounding happens to most people between the ages of preverbal to about 10 years of age and that's when we are forming all our beliefs about who we are in the world. Shaping our identity by how others see and treat us. The problem is that we also take on limiting beliefs very early in life, beliefs we make about ourselves in the world due to what's happening to us or happening around us. Many people's wounded parts take on something about feeling defective or wrong or not okay and those beliefs tend to stick around unless we begin to uncover them in coaching or therapy. Those limiting beliefs have all been collected and collated in our wounded child part, the little me, and it hurts a lot when those beliefs get activated. Ingeniously, another older part who comes along at 11/12 or 13 years of age wants to cover up that little wounded part and begins to protect it, defend it, or avoid it, so it doesn't have to feel it so much, hence it starts adapting and doing lots of other things to push away those feelings, including numbing, soothing, and dissociating from ourselves.

When I work with clients, I will always explain a parts model to them and how they are made up of at least three parts: their adult, their adapted self, and their wounded self. The job is to try over time to separate out their adult "I" self from their younger parts. Then they can see how their adult self hasn't really been in the driving seat, their adapted self has, and it's been beating up mostly on the wounded self and that's not going to work moving forwards. It sounds like an oxymoron, but we must separate out first and "un-blend" the parts to then integrate them further down the line. This reduces an awful lot of shame and blame and helps someone to see that all their parts, in different ways, have been trying to help or protect them.

My role is to help them begin to recognise where their "I" is in the moment, what their adult thinks and feels, and whether what is happening for them is activating their adapted or their wounded part. Moving towards curiosity and compassion, them beginning to speak to those parts and re-parent them from their adult, healing their younger selves and trusting their adult self in the process. People who are predominantly in their adult selves make much better leaders and therapists! They can also step back, observe, start to notice when everybody else is in their adapted and wounded parts, but without becoming activated themselves and able to stay in their own adult.

A Conversation With Lou Lebentz

Lisa So, if we're thinking about the future, what's next in trauma-informed care? What's next for you in that leadership space? Where do you see the future now?

Lou I think that we are living in an increasingly traumatised society and space now due to global issues and political instability. There's a lot going on in the world that means people find themselves either constantly in hyper-arousal and hyper-vigilant, or in hypo-arousal and freeze response. They are dissociated, disconnected, and dysregulated. When someone disconnects because their nervous system is dysregulated, they are not only no longer in their body or somatic system but also, they are also disconnected from their heart. Our heart is very much the seat of someone's spiritual and soul self, which is not a good idea to be disengaged from. So, I think it's imperative we think about how we reconnect people back up to their body and their feelings. Because otherwise they can't reconnect to their hearts. Humanity as a race must become more heart-centred and recognise that we have to lead the world from a place of compassion and understanding and not from a place of disconnection, dysregulation, and fear.

We also need to get trauma and trauma-informed care far more out there into the mainstream, but we need to do that with the right level of training and monitoring as well. Because another challenge is there's also a bit of a backlash in the mental health arena with many practitioners or clinics/treatment spaces professing to be trauma-informed when they are not. Trauma-informed cannot be used as a marketing ploy and gained in a webinar or day's training. You could be trauma-aware but using the term *informed* on profiles; websites have become a bit of a tick box exercise and I think we need to be extremely mindful who and what is trauma-informed because with it there is an perception of depth.

Lisa It's a huge problem.

Lou And all of us that are in this space, in my mind, need to collaborate so that we can start to put programmes, trainings, and awareness into different sectors because people need this knowledge, they need this awareness, they need to understand where most mental health struggles and not just mental health struggles, world struggles, come from.

Because we wouldn't be witnessing what we are in the world if some of the world leaders weren't coming from a grossly traumatised place, having done absolutely no work on themselves. Hence, we are experiencing an awful lot of adapted leaders behaving like teenagers, with terribly hurt wounded inner children running countries and governments and industries. With no adults on board whatsoever. Rigidly, harmfully, and unconsciously ruling the world and hurting people because they're not looking at their own stuff, which leaves us very much concluding the vital importance of focusing on our own wellness, our own history, our own recovery, and our own understanding of where we've been and who we are now.

People, whomever they are, must do the work; every one of us has got to swim towards the dark, and dive into the sublime but scary seas. Whether it's Dante's Inferno or the Belly of the Whale or the archetypal Hero's Journey, there is no getting away from ourselves and we as human beings must travel inwards.

In my experience with almost everyone I've worked with over the last 20 years, including myself, the journey or the Voyage is about going internally, starting to meet those wounded and adapted parts and finally make friends with them. We must learn to integrate the wounds, so they hurt no longer. Start to love and accept ourselves. But to do that, we must be courageous, and go there ourselves in order to encourage others to come along with us.

Reflection

I would have been surprised were I to have been in conversation with a psychotherapist who did not start from the premise that "it starts with me." That said, it is important that it is not assumed that someone is engaged in their own healing journey and therefore robust mechanisms must be in place in settings, services, and systems to ensure that every opportunity is available to develop and heal such as clinical supervision, group coaching, and space for self-care and well-being.

Discussion Points

1. **Importance of Awareness and Education**
   - How can the psychotherapy field improve education and awareness around trauma?
   - What strategies can be employed to ensure that practitioners are knowledgeable about trauma and its impacts?
2. **Role of Personal History in Professional Practice**
   - In what ways do personal experiences and family dynamics influence one's approach to caregiving and therapy?
   - How can clinicians manage over-responsibility and set healthy boundaries?

3. **Personal Healing and Professional Development**
   - How does personal healing contribute to professional effectiveness in therapy?
   - What are the benefits of programmes like the Voyage® in supporting clinicians' growth?
4. **Application of the Parts Model in Therapy**
   - What are the advantages of using a parts model in trauma therapy?
   - How can this model help clients understand and integrate their different selves?
5. **Effective Leadership and Emotional Regulation**
   - Why is it important for leaders and therapists to stay in their adult selves?
   - How can effective leadership be fostered in trauma-informed care settings?
6. **Future Directions for Trauma-Informed Care**
   - What are the next steps for advancing trauma-informed care in society?
   - How can trauma-informed practices be more widely implemented in different sectors?
7. **Challenges and Misuse of Trauma-Informed Labels**
   - How can the mental health field address the misuse of the trauma-informed label?
   - What measures can be taken to ensure that trauma-informed care is delivered authentically and effectively?
8. **Global and Societal Impact of Trauma**
   - How does trauma at the leadership level affect society as a whole?
   - What role does personal wellness and recovery play in broader societal change?

References

Berne, A. (1971). *Layman's Guide to Psychiatry and Psychoanalysis*. Penguin.

Felitti, V. J., Anda, R. F., Nordenberg, D., Williamson, D. F., Spitz, A. M., Edwards, V., Koss, M. P., & Marks, J. S. (1998, May). Relationship of childhood abuse and household dysfunction to many of the leading causes of death in adults. The adverse childhood experiences (ACE) study. *American Journal of Preventive Medicine*, 14(4), 245–258.

14
A Conversation With Amelia Brunt

A Strengths-based Lens on the Menopause

In this chapter we explore the interconnected relationship between burnout and menopause in the helping professions and consider the huge potential for both individuals and organisations when menopause is viewed through a strengths-based leadership lens. This chapter is for everyone, whether you have been through menopause, are in the throes of menopause, years away from menopause, or will never go through menopause due to the biology of your birth-assigned gender. It is for everyone because we all live and work with the 50% of people who will experience menopause at some point in their life. The global population of postmenopausal women is expected to continue growing, with projections estimating that by 2025, there will be around 1.1 billion postmenopausal women worldwide.[1]

We also want to make a note about language; in this chapter we have used the term "woman" to refer to a person who experiences or has experienced menstruation. We respectfully recognise that there may be people reading this chapter who do not identify with the gender assigned to them at birth. In fact, for gender-diverse people with a womb the challenges of menopause can be significantly more complex (Toze & Westwood, 2024). So, in the interests of avoiding complex and extended phraseology, please note that by "women" we mean women and people who bleed or who have bled. That is to say that we fully recognise the complexity of the issues, even if they are not mentioned here. This chapter refers to the particular cross-sectionality of menstruation, working in the helping professions and then going through menopause and the experiences of overwhelm and burnout that this can reveal. In addition to the complexity of this cross-sectionality are factors such as neurodiversity, gender diversity, race, poverty, addiction, living with domestic abuse, and histories of early life trauma, for example, which are known to exacerbate the experiences of people going through menopause but which we will not necessarily cover here.

Lisa So tell me how you arrived to be working with educators, leadership, and the menopause.

Amelia I was a classroom teacher during the 1990s and 2000s and then in 2008 I moved into working with children looked after.[2] The pastoral and well-being piece had always been important to me as a vehicle towards children doing well at school.

I worked for a long time, supporting schools, thinking about children's needs, operating within a very systemic model alongside social care and therapeutic services. I loved it. However, increasingly, as happens when you're engaged in this work, I noticed over time that it is also the adults around the children who need the support to support the children.

A lot of my work at the time centred around training and supervision for staff through my role at the Virtual School. However, as budgets reduced and the number of children in care and in crisis increased, the role gradually changed, and I felt that there was less opportunity to support the staff in schools in the way that was needed. I felt passionate about the necessity of that aspect of my work. At the same time, running alongside that, I'd been doing the job for many years and as you know, Lisa, being exposed to traumatic content over a long period of time can take its toll without the right support around you. So, I was seeing that there were people in school who needed more support, emotionally and psychologically, while at the same time recognising that in the role I was in, I needed this too.

During that time supervision in schools was a relatively new idea and because I was employed on teachers' pay and conditions, it wasn't felt that this was something I was entitled to in my role, despite the level of vicarious trauma I was exposed to. I just knew something had to change, both for myself and for others.

In hindsight, I can now see that this level of overwhelm and burnout was at the height of my own menopause experience. I decided to seek out a deeper understanding of clinical supervision. I trained and qualified at postgraduate level, providing me with the academic underpinnings, while at the same time taking Bruce Perry's Neurosequential Model of Reflective Supervision[3] training, which applied the trauma-informed lens that I was looking for. I left my role in education and started working directly with educators and other professionals who work with traumatised children: educational psychologists, therapists, and domestic abuse support workers, for example.

As I offered supervision, consolidating all my own training and experience, while at the same time riding out my own menopause process, I started to recognise that all of my knowledge about nervous system regulation and polyvagal theory (Porges, 2011) was so needed and so relevant here. Everything I'd learned over the years around supporting people to be aware of their nervous system, and their window of tolerance. The impact of early life attachment experiences, the level of trauma people had experienced and been exposed to. It was all interconnected with how challenging the menopause process was for people.

The Nervous System

By nervous system we are referring the autonomic nervous system (ANS), that is the part of the nervous system which is automatic and away from our conscious awareness. The ANS plays a crucial role in maintaining homeostasis, which is the body's ability to maintain a stable internal environment, as well as emotional stability, despite external changes. It ensures that vital functions are carried out efficiently and adapts to the body's needs in different situations through its different branches. Crucially, when the body is over stressed for long periods of time, we experience this as "dysregulation"; our nervous system is struggling to maintain balance, both physically and emotionally. We move outside of our window of tolerance, and may require the support of others, or known regulation strategies to help us move back into a balanced state (Dana, 2021).

The menopause was wreaking havoc with my nervous system at this time and so, as is my way, I started to explore more around this. While we live in amazing times in terms of how much more access we have to information about the menopause and how many more opportunities we have to talk about it, I felt like there was more to it than just that which was being talked about in the mainstream media. I understood about hormones, hot flushes, sleep disturbance, and impact on word retrieval, for example, but from a psychological point of view, what was happening? My background was originally in psychological enquiry with a BSc in Social Psychology, and so that was how I approached thinking about this menopause journey, and it felt very much like a journey, to an unknown destination; I wasn't sure what I would find when I got there.

What I did find through my research and studies was a whole body of work around menopause that I had no idea existed, from academics and various people who've studied the menstrual cycle and menopause for years and years and in great depth. Dr Lara Owen,[4] Dr Sharon Blackie,[5] Alexandra Pope, and Sjanie Hugo-Wurlitzer,[6] for example. It was through this work that I learnt a different view of menopause and the connection between menopause and self-leadership and leadership in the world. We could think of this as an opportunity for postmenopausal growth, which I would never have believed could be a thing until I read the research. It gave me a far better understanding of my own experience and of the experiences of the people I was working with.

Lisa   So tell me about that different lens on menopause. What does that look like for you in your work?

Amelia   My work now is very much focussed on burnout prevention, recovery, and growth. I think most of us are starting to understand more about our hormones and the symptoms of menopause but that's a very medical model and there's a sense that women have something wrong with their health when these symptoms appear. When you go through menopause, it's seen as a health crisis and it can feel like a health crisis, without the deeper information around the purpose of this psychological change and development.

I felt there was something else going on and that something else, which I was exposed to through my research, was that actually the reason in our society that menopause is so hard for so many people is that by the time we get there, many of us, especially in the helping professions, are completely burnt out.

Lisa There is a really important observation here about language; the term "health crisis" brings very different emotions to the fore than thinking about purpose and change and development.

Amelia Exactly, because menopause, when viewed through a strengths-based lens, is an initiation into the next phase of our life. So, both an ending and a beginning. An ending of one phase of our lives (and any woman who's been through the menopause will recognise that feeling), and with endings comes a huge sense of loss and grief. But also, a beginning of the next very valuable phase, valuable to ourselves as individuals, but also valuable to the systems we live and work in and to us as leaders in the world. I'm thinking here about postmenopausal leaders in the climate change awareness field, taking a stand for the world, people like 77-year-old climate activist Gaie Delap,[7] for example.

There is a lot of thinking about what have I achieved? What else did I want to achieve? And importantly, what doesn't serve me well anymore? What do I need to change now for this next phase of my life? If we are not aware of the psychological processes of menopause, we risk blowing everything up and maybe regretting that in the future. People leave long-term partners, leave jobs, fall out with their adult children or parents, or friends, for example, without a reflective lens around the process that they might be in. I'm not saying these things shouldn't happen, but the trauma-informed practitioner in me likes to be curious and lean towards doing things with a felt sense of safety rather than the reactivity that burnout and menopause can cause. Through the work of people like Alexandra Pope from Red School[8] whose organisation has really dedicated many, many years to studying what they call "Menstrual Cycle Awareness and Conscious Menopause" and through my own work at Well Educated,[9] we see a similar psychological process unfolding in everyone who goes through menopause: an unsettling, a sense of wanting to withdraw from the world, a period of review, reflection, and healing and then ultimately a rebirth, a new beginning—the wise woman. It might not be an easy journey, and of course for many of us it is not, but there is gold at the end. It is not a case of the best years of your life are over. In actual fact the best is yet to come, and I never would have believed that when I was going through the process.

Lisa So there's quite a lot in there to unpack, but if we're thinking about how organisations care for the people who care, it strikes me that the model that you're referring to is very, very far away from how organisations might view the menopause and what that might mean for caring for that workforce.

Because let's face it, education, children's services, therapy, psychotherapy, play therapy, drama therapy, you know, these are all settings, services, and systems that are predominantly female workforces.

I guess what I want to explore is what good practice looks like? Does good practice incorporate the model you're describing and what does it look like if we don't have good practice?

Amelia A lot of my work is around vicarious trauma, secondary traumatic stress, overwhelm, burnout, and organisations are really having to face up to these realities. We know out there, in the field, that organisations are facing retention and recruitment challenges, sickness rates are really high, and we are really seeing a physical and mental health crisis in the helping professions. Without the right knowledge and support around them, people are burnt out by their work, and burnout in the helping professions is for me a safeguarding risk. One of the key features of burnout according to Maslach's Burnout Inventory (Maslach, 2020) is the depersonalisation that people experience and this dramatically effects decision-making. When decisions are being made about people's lives, this is a safeguarding risk. So, it is important that individuals and organisations have a good understanding of burnout, of the hierarchical nature of the nervous system, the connection between well-being and effective service delivery, and be able to nurture that from an individual point of view, but also collectively. That's the starting point, I think. And then onto that, we can piggy-back the fact that the majority of the people who work in this sector, these sectors, these helping professions, are people who will one day go through the menopause process which by its very nature disrupts the nervous system and well-being.

We can ignore that at our peril because what's happening currently is people are retiring early or leaving in their 40s and 50s, or being off work for extended periods of time, or not feeling like they are doing a good job when they are there. We know through mental health research that job satisfaction is a key requirement for good mental health and the risks of moral injury through work are greater during the menopause years (Brent et al., 2015; Converso et al., 2019). But actually, if we can incorporate some better understanding around the process and what's happening, there's gold in that for individuals, for service users, and for organisations as well.

Lisa Let's get to the gold in a minute because actually there has been a crisis in the workplace that's been well documented regarding people leaving work in their 50s post-COVID (ONS, 2022). Unfortunately, the ONS study does not ask any questions directly about the menopause but it does talk about mental health and physical health as factors. It would be really interesting to see whether asking the question about the menopause as a factor for leaving the workplace made a difference as I think it well might.

Amelia No, the ONS study sadly didn't ask directly about menopause, but there are other studies which have addressed that very question (DWP, 2023, 2024; CIPD, 2023). The CIPD surveyed over 2,000 women, aged 40 to 60, currently employed in the UK and who could be experiencing menopause transition and found that around one in six (17%) of workers surveyed reported considering leaving their job due to lack of support with their menopause symptoms and 6% have left work for this reason. Also, the Fawcett Society, a UK charity campaigning for gender equality and women's rights, estimated that one in ten women, aged between 40 and 55, working through menopause have left a job because of their symptoms and a further 13% reported that they had considered leaving (Bazeley et al., 2022). It is very much on the government's agenda to retain the skillsets of the menopausing workforce.

Lisa   It might be worth outlining some of the symptoms of menopause at this point so that we can have an understanding about how it might show up in the workplace. Fortunately, for me, my symptoms were quite manageable. But being more specific in our use of medical terminology, and let's define what we're talking about here, we're talking actually about perimenopause, aren't we, and that period of perimenopause where people talk a lot about feeling more anxious, feeling more tired, putting on weight, having incredibly intrusive bleeds. . .

Amelia   Bleeds that are unpredictable, the loss of that cyclical predictability that we've had all our lives.

Lisa   Those symptoms alone, when working with trauma and adversity and pressure and a lack of resources . . . is it any wonder that the menopausing workforce may well have decided, I don't want to go back into that, this is a time for me to withdraw?

Whereas actually, what I think you're wanting to bring to the fore is that this is a period of time that if we utilise it well in the workforce, we can really create, nurture, develop something quite special and different.

Amelia   Yes. Leadership in every sense of the word.

Obviously, there's the medical definition of menopause which is the date one year after your final bleed but what we're talking about when we use the word *menopause* here is the process that is ongoing for a number of years. For some women that can be up to 10 years, though I believe the average is between two and seven years. It's a long time and it's a long time in a person's working life and part of that process is the need to withdraw. It's like the snow globe has been shaken. What we could cope with in the past may now be overwhelming. Women often report "I can't listen to the news, I can't engage with it, I just don't want to know about what's happening anymore. I just need some peace and quiet and downtime." And so, yes, we will retreat from work, especially when we work in organisations where we're on the frontline dealing with, through social care, through education, with traumatic content and experiences. It is the perfect storm of empathy fatigue, physical and mental exhaustion, and a sense that we have lost our mojo, so to speak.

So, I do feel strongly, that there's an individual responsibility to learn more about this whole process, because I had no idea. But also culturally, there is a need for a shift towards better recognising the impact of working in the helping professions on our female nervous systems, particularly during this extended period of change that we call perimenopause and menopause.

For me, in my work, the menopause burnout piece fits together like a jigsaw piece with the general burnout piece. So, part of the solution to not just surviving but eventually thriving in the menopause process is about nurturing our individual and collective nervous systems, understanding polyvagal theory specifically in relation to the less talked about female cyclical nature.

Lisa Let's expand on the relevance of polyvagal theory here . . .

Amelia Yes, the work of Stephen Porges (Porges, 2011), as we know, has had a huge and beneficial influence on our understanding of trauma and the body's stress response system. Polyvagal theory has given us both a framework of understanding and a road map towards better social engagement. In addition to this, the work of people like Peter Levine and Somatic Experiencing (Levine, 1997), Bruce Perry's Neurosequential Model (Perry & Graner, 2018), and Dan Siegel's Interpersonal Neurobiology (Siegel, 2012) have all contributed to a better understanding of nervous system regulation and dysregulation and how we can support ourselves and each other to be in the best place to be well and do well. However, after years of being immersed in this work, what is clear to me is the missing piece, that cycles are also important to nervous system regulation; human beings, like all other species on the planet, are cyclical beings and the cycles we live in and that are within us affect our innate needs and therefore our well-being at any given time.

Lisa How do you think that understanding cycles and what really happens in the menopause, how can that help women who work in the helping professions and how can that help the organisations that those women work in?

Amelia Any woman who tracks the emotional landscape of their menstrual cycle will know that their mood and energies change with the cycle, that there is a pattern to this and that it is very predictable. Indeed, all of us are familiar with the different mood and energies we have with the changing seasons over a year, for example. However, there is no recognition of this in our mainstream culture, and yet all of us and particularly women are experiencing life within these cycles while either ignoring their existence or labelling them as some sort of mental health issue: premenstrual syndrome or seasonal affective disorder, for example. This does something very particular to us, to our identities, and to our nervous systems, particularly during menopause. You and I, Lisa, we're both very, very passionate about the language used and what language means for people and what I hear repeatedly in workplaces are sentences like, "Oh, I'm sorry, I'm just having a menopause moment" or, "Oh god, sorry, menopause brain fog" and that's not to say these aren't a thing, because of course they are, but by using this reductionist language, we reduce this process to a mental health issue rather than the phenomenal period of transformation and potential that it is.

Lisa I love that articulation and distinction between reducing the menopause to a medical process rather than one of deep transformation into wisdom.

Amelia Working in the helping professions requires regular and consistent self-care and organisational care if people are going to continue to deliver these services. We know a good-quality service is trauma informed and responsive, that it is person centred and focussed on felt safety, consistency, and trust and one way we can access all of these values and practices is to bring in the additional awareness of cyclicity. This links to the role and importance of interoception, so difficult for so many in our western industrialised culture, and very much more difficult for those who experience neurodiversity (Gottardello & Steffan, 2024): being able to listen to the body and understand what it is telling us. And this is absolutely crucial in the menopause process if we are to understand it as a journey of transformational change and growth which can benefit the individual, the organisation, and the world, rather than a health crisis and the end of life as we know it.

> **Interoception**
>
> Interoception is one of our less talked about senses. It is the sense that allows us to perceive the internal state of our body and requires a level of conscious awareness that is brought about through positive and co-regulating attachment relationships in our earliest months and years. Interoception also requires a degree of neurotypicality and those who are neurodiverse report particular challenges with this sense. Interoception involves sensing signals from internal organs, such as the gut, heart, and lungs, and integrating these signals into our conscious and subconscious awareness. This process is crucial for maintaining homeostasis and self-awareness. Brain and body are not separate, however, and therefore interoceptive awareness also links to psychological awareness and well-being. Research has shown that greater interoceptive awareness is associated with better emotional regulation and mental health.[10]

Lisa How does it help?

Amelia Tuning in to our natural rhythms and cycles is by its very nature an act of interoception. I can speak from personal experience, and I can speak in relation to the people that I've worked with and I would say that, for me, there was a huge sense of Now what? How do I live like this? When I understood menopause from a different perspective, a much more strengths-based perspective, with something at the end of it that was for the world, that spoke to me. I've got more to give and knowing this enabled me to move more towards, standing in my power, you know, standing as a wiser older woman with a much wider and longer lens on the world, on my work, and on myself.

It was a bit like when you first learn about trauma-informed practice and you can't look at the world in the old way anymore. You can't see the world through a behaviourist lens anymore, because once you know and understand the impact of trauma on people and behaviour, that's the only way you can view it. It was like that, when I originally learned about the nervous system and the biological hierarchies of brain and body, it made so much sense, I just knew it to be true. It is the same for menstruation and menopause; we have been told a different story by the society we live in, but the old story is still there, it is in our bodies, our blood and bones, our DNA. We know we are cyclical and we know the menopause process is about change and growth when we become aware of it again. Our ancestors knew this, and many indigenous cultures still know this and so I think there is strength in having this different story for women and for women to hear this different story.

There is self-compassion in it, there is understanding of yourself and others and there is hope that there is something else at the other side. If we lose everybody because they are burnt out, who's got all that knowledge and experience of life in the helping professions? We don't just lose a person. We lose so much more, and I've always felt that; people go, and we lose their knowledge and expertise, their wisdom. One of the things that menopause does for us is it enables us to see such a broader picture and that is really precious and valuable to organisations. People who've got a balanced wisdom about what might need to happen for organisations, systems, families, people young and old, whatever service it is.

Lisa And also there's something for me that wants to ask who are the mentors going to be? Because if we have a workforce that doesn't have those women over 50 on the other side of menopause with all that that brings, then who mentors the younger people?

I ask this because I specifically remember when I was in my 20s, I saw women in their 40s and 50s who held spaces, who shone a light on that which I was yet to understand, who offered guidance. I very much remember the social worker in the team next to ours who asked me if I was okay when I came back from maternity leave because she could see damn well that I wasn't. Those women who are now us can offer that mentorship.

I'm going to become/will have become a grandmother in April and the thing that's really struck me is that I had children, like everybody else, before I had deep wisdom! How interesting it is that nature allows us to do that, but I think it allows us to do that because there has to be space for the grandma.

Amelia Historically we didn't live in such isolated ways where someone has a baby and then is left all day on their own in their house to raise that baby. There would have been a whole community of wise women who could help a woman (and men) to learn how to raise a baby. There is a reason why humans continue to live a long while after childbearing ends, and the reason is that these women had much to offer the tribe and its survival. Menopause gives us an evolutionary edge.

There are believed to be only three animals that continue to have a valuable role to play post menopause, orca whales, gall-forming aphids, and humans (Codrington, 2022). Professor Darren Croft and his team at the University of Exeter, having watched and researched the orca (killer) whale extensively, have noted that postmenopausal female orca have the role of mentoring the young male orca (Brent et al., 2015). The young male orca joins up with a wiser older female for a number of years while she teaches him how to hunt and how to be a successfully surviving orca. Species such as orca and humans wouldn't have survived without the wisdom of the older female and I think that's exactly what you're saying about services, Lisa, where there's a lot too that is still really valuable and could be protected if we nurtured and respected it.

Lisa I really want to ask you about what good practice you've seen, what would be the gold standard, but I'm thinking, because this is such a new area, that it would actually be really difficult to have seen that in practice. So, with that in mind. If we could dream gold star practice, what would that look like?

Amelia My work is with individuals through coaching and groups through training and keynote speaking so I'm not involved in service development and delivery so much. However, gold star practice for me always comes back to nervous system regulation and wellness: how we support our people in our services and who deliver our services, but also how we educate them with a better understanding of their unique nervous system and the impact of the nervous systems around us. Many, many people who work in the helping professions have their own lived experience of early life trauma and attachment disruption, for example. They do this work because it resonates with them, and they want to be and to make the difference that they never had. However, this also adds to the risk and vulnerability of overwhelm, burnout, and vicarious trauma. Part of the solution to this is the psychoeducation around it.

I would like to see us build and share knowledge for everybody, not just for women. Everybody lives, works, is related to somebody with a womb, who goes through this process, whether it's your sister, your wife, your mum, your colleague, your boss, whoever it is and so everybody needs this understanding not just of the physical change that is happening, but also of all that is happening psychologically.

A lot of the physical symptoms of menopause are worse because of the lifestyles we've led within the society and culture that we live and work in. It's like the perfect storm by 50. We're exhausted, we've raised families, our parents might now be ill, our children still need us, our jobs and all the other roles we play continue to be incredibly demanding; it really is the perfect storm. On top of this are the financial pressures of the cost of living and the systemic irregularities of race, gender, religion, and sexuality, for example. At the same time our nervous systems are saying to us to slow down, it's time to reflect and take stock, to learn what we want to do next in the world, to heal from the life we have led, so that we can still be of value to our community, so we can be leaders in whatever form that may take.

Lisa You're really speaking to how multilayered this is: our own lived experiences, our own living experiences, working for years around adversity and trauma and then the menopause. That's quite a life of experience that requires a lot of understanding how that all works together.

Amelia Yes, the result of all of this is that we're much more susceptible to burnout and we are also much more susceptible to a really challenging menopause process and so there's something about helping people to access this different lens to view their experience and the experiences of those around them. My work with individuals and with organisations focusses on naming and recognising these vulnerabilities to secondary traumatic stress and vicarious trauma and ensuring that our processes and practices support people to both prevent and recover from burnout and menopausal burnout. It's a privilege to work with so many who have lived a life and have so much to offer the world in their leadership roles now, no matter how big or small they might feel that leadership role in the world is. When the menopause process has been honoured and understood in this way, postmenopausal growth is a huge asset to us as individuals, to our communities, our organisations, and to our ever changing world.

Lisa So this chapter, because the subject matter is so new, strikes me as an invitation, an invitation for people to individually think about the menopause and lived experience and trauma and working with trauma and adversity, but also for organisations to consider what this all means for better service delivery and best practice.

That is so they can consider how they can better ensure the well-being of those women, of those people experiencing menopause. So that they can step into more roles, more focused around mentorship, leadership, and coaching relationships.

Reflection

Shifting the thinking out of the medical model into thinking about this period of time as a natural, holistic movement into a period of wisdom can feel quite challenging, not least because it has taken so long to talk about the menopause at all! My hope is that there can be a much better understanding in the workforce and that the fruits of this cycle are harnessed rather than sidelined, leaving many incredibly experienced practitioners to leave their place of work.

Discussion Points

1. **Addressing Vicarious Trauma and Burnout**
   - Why has there been a growing need for organisations to address vicarious trauma, secondary traumatic stress, and burnout among their staff, particularly in the helping professions?
   - How much understanding do you have about the importance of understanding and nurturing nervous system well-being?
2. **Menopause and Work**
   - The process of menopause, which can last several years, impacts many women in the workforce, especially in helping professions. How much is known in your organisation about the impact of the menopause?
   - Menopause often involves psychological changes that can lead to frustration and withdrawal, necessitating better understanding and support within organisations. How might these psychological changes impact practice?

3. **Cycle Awareness**
   - In what ways is your organisation increasing awareness of menstrual cycles and the menopause process? What role do you have to ensure that this awareness becomes more recognised, ensuring a progressive organisation?
   - How can understanding these processes help to reduce stigma, allow emotional and physical well-being, and support women through different phases of their lives?
4. **Integrating Menopause and Burnout Solutions**
   - Addressing menopause and burnout together involves nurturing the nervous system and incorporating polyvagal theory into support strategies. What can be learnt about the nervous system that would help learning?
   - Could recognising the interconnectedness of these issues lead to more comprehensive support systems for women? In what way?
5. **Strength-Based Perspective on Menopause**
   - Can viewing menopause from a strengths-based perspective empower women by highlighting its potential for growth and wisdom?
   - Can this perspective foster self-compassion, understanding, and hope for a positive future?
6. **Impact on Organisations**
   - Does the departure of seasoned female employees due to menopause and burnout result in a considerable loss of expertise and mentorship within organisations?
   - Can providing support for these women strengthen organisational resilience and offer valuable guidance for younger employees?
7. **Holistic Approach**
   - How does a holistic employee well-being strategy combine knowledge of trauma, lived experiences, and systemic issues?

- What shared responsibilities do individuals and organisations have in this context?
8. **Supporting Menopause with Compassion in the Workplace**
   - What reasonable adjustments might be helpful for someone navigating perimenopause or menopause, and how do I approach these conversations collaboratively?
   - How can I contribute to a workplace culture where being safe, seen, soothed, and secure is the norm for all staff, especially during vulnerable life stages?

Notes

1. https://menomartha.com/health-topic/postmenopause-statistics/.
2. Children looked after refers to children who are in the care of the local authority. Sometimes the term looked-after children is used or children can be referred to as children in care.
3. www.neurosequential.com.
4. Dr Lara Owen has researched and consulted globally on menstruation, menopause, women's well-being, and women's rights. She teaches courses at the postgraduate level on Contemporary Menstrual Studies. Further information can be found on her website: www.laraowen.com.
5. Dr Sharon Blackie, writer and psychologist, has taught and lectured at several academic institutions. Further information can be found at www.sharonblackie.net.
6. Alexandra Pope and Sjanie Hugo-Wurlitzer are the co-founders of Red School, and have developed a radical new approach to health, creativity, leadership, and spiritual life based on the power of the menstrual cycle. www.redschool.net.
7. Taylor, D. (2024, December 21). Elderly activist to spend Christmas in prison because tag does not fit. *The Guardian*, accessed on 8th January 2025.
8. www.redschool.net.
9. www.well-educated.co.uk.
10. www.frontiersin.org.

References

Bazeley, A., Marren, C., & Shepherd, A. (2022). *Menopause and the Workplace*. The Fawcett Society. www.fawcettsociety.org.uk, accessed on 4th January 2025.

Brent, L. J. N., Franks, D. W., Foster, E. A., Balcomb, K. C., Cant, M. A., & Croft, D. P. (2015). Ecological knowledge, leadership, and the evolution of menopause in killer whales. *Current Biology*, 25(6), 746–750.

Chartered Institute of Personnel and Development (CIPD). (2023). *Menopause in the Workplace: Employee Experiences in 2023*. CIPD, accessed on 4th January 2025.

Codrington, K. (2022). *Second Spring*. HarperCollins Publishers.

Converso, D., Viotti, S., Sottimano, I., Loera, B., Molinengo, G., & Guidetti, G. (2019). The relationship between menopausal symptoms and burnout. A cross-sectional study among nurses. *BMC Women's Health*, 19, 1–12.

Dana, D. (2021). *Anchored: How to Befriend Your Nervous System Using Polyvagal Theory*. Sounds True.

Department for Work and Pensions (DWP). (2023). *No Time to Step Back: The Government's Menopause Employment Champion*. GOV.UK, accessed on 5th January 2025.

Department for Work and Pensions (DWP). (2024). *Shattering the Silence about Menopause: 12-Month Progress Report*. GOV.UK, accessed on 5th January 2025.

Gottardello, D., & Steffan, B. (2024). Fundamental intersectionality of menopause and neurodivergence experiences at work. *Maturitas*, 189, 1–6. Article ID 108107.

Levine, P. A. (1997). *Waking the Tiger: Healing Trauma*. North Atlantic Books.

Maslach, C. (2020). https://different.hr/wp-content/uploads/2020/05/Maslach-Burnout-Inventory-MBI.pdf, accessed on 4th January 2025.

Office of National Statistics (ONS). (2022). *Reasons for Workers Aged Over 50 Years Leaving Employment Since the Start of the Coronavirus Pandemic: Wave 2*. ONS Website.

Perry, B. D., & Graner, S. (2018). *The Neurosequential Model in Education: Introduction to the NME Series: Trainer's Guide (NME Training Guide)*. The ChildTrauma Academy Press.

Porges, S. W. (2011). *The Polyvagal Theory: Neurophysiological Foundations of Emotions, Attachment, Communication, and Self-Regulation*. W. W. Norton & Co.

Siegel, D. J. (2012). *Pocket Guide to Interpersonal Neurobiology: An Integrative Handbook of the Mind*. W. W. Norton & Company.
Toze, M., & Westwood, S. (2024). Experiences of menopause among non-binary and trans people. *International Journal of Transgender Health*, 26(2), 447–458.

15
A Conversation With Lisa Lea Weston
Why Supervision Is Essential

This chapter will explore the relationship between supervision and caring for the workforce and why that is vital, particularly in trauma-informed settings. We will look at the importance of senior leaders being in supervision and how that supports both them and how they are able to undertake their role in service of the children and young people in their settings and how it establishes a culture which can safeguard children and young people. A culture that Debbie Innes-Turnill refers to in her book, *Safeguarding in the Classroom*, which looks broadly and holistically at safeguarding. We will explore how vital the relationship is with a trained supervisor and how it fundamentally can help prevent compassion fatigue and staff burnout. We also think about how supervision allows vital space for reflection on the system, both organisationally and more widely in society, the world and how this impacts our capacity to work.

Lisa C   So let's start with exploring the relationship between caring for the workforce and supervision and how that shows itself.

Lisa L-W   For me, apart from management structures and a supportive workplace culture that is established, supervision is fundamental to the work of caring for the workforce. I've learned over the years through working in NHS and other settings, that it is senior leaders who set the tone and culture of what happens in those workplaces.

If we work in service of other human beings, then there are always all kinds of feelings and thoughts and power dynamics that are flowing around that usually don't get reflected upon; they just get responded to and people are then responsive to each other's

> Supervision is recommended to anyone working in roles that require regularly giving or receiving emotionally challenging communications, or engaging in relationally complex and challenging roles.
>
> BACP Ethical Framework

fight/flight/freeze/flop/fawn survival responses. Supervision is the only formal process that holds accountability for best practice for the beneficiary (children in education) and the well-being of the practitioner/educator as dynamically connected.

Lisa C   You now lead an organisation that is entirely focused on delivering supervision to senior leaders within education. That's not your background. What is your background? And what was the journey that you took from where you were in your career to leading this organisation?

Lisa L-W   I've always worked with children and young people since my Duke of Edinburgh award; in fact, on reflection, that award was important because I remember going into a residential setting for children with a learning disability and looking around at the adults to see how to do things, to learn, and what I saw was the adults tying children down and force-feeding them, in the early 1990s. I remember feeling with all of my being, why is that okay? How are these adults who seem "nice" in interactions I have with them doing this? This is where I began when I was 15 years old. I was appalled by what I saw and over the years that has stayed with me.

I spent 10 years in the NHS working with adults with profound and multiple learning disabilities and in acute adult mental health. I now realise this is where I learnt much more about the importance of supporting a network around a person. The people I worked with in the NHS needed ongoing support to make therapeutic change. Confidentiality had to be held differently. It was no good working with a person in drama therapy and seeing amazing change, for example, in relation to expressing feelings about current or historic abuse. It needed to be sensitively understood by those that cared for them. Myself and my multidisciplinary team developed differing ways of working with key workers and importantly the leaders of care settings that our "patients" lived in. Without them understanding the role of the NHS therapy provision, little could change. We undertook many ways of trying to consistently reach and communicate with residential settings and this often included inviting them to experience a version of some of the group sensory sessions we undertook. This idea has filtered into the way of working that now exists at Talking Heads.

I continued a private practice with children and young people whilst in the NHS. I was a young drama therapist. Originally when I qualified, I was 23; I'm now 51. I didn't train as a supervisor until four years post qualifying.

I have always had my own supervision with someone from a different discipline and I attend supervision twice per month due to the scope and complexity of the work I hold.

I left the NHS after nearly 10 years as I was exhausted; I had a year's treatment for breast cancer and the NHS was unable to accommodate my psychological need for a phased return (they did accommodate a phased return for my physical needs). I have written about fluctuations in fitness to practise with colleagues, Dr. Ditty Dokter and Tara Thornewood. I essentially left the NHS wondering how I would do my best work in a system that struggled to support clinicians to do that as the focus was solely on what would be good for the person we were seeing without acknowledging the support staff needed to perform well and humanely.

I retained a small ongoing drama therapy and supervisory practice whilst in the NHS. I worked freelance in several primary schools as a therapist and supervisor, in private practice as well as delivering sessions for The Adoption Consultancy 360, and the Kinship team for the local council. A throwaway comment by a head teacher where he said, "imagine how many children's lives you could change, if you just did that supervision thing that you do with this counsellor here, with all of us head teachers."

I thought, yes. This is the other way to support the children and young people that I work with. By supporting the system. I am trained predominantly in the Shohet and Hawkins seven-eyed model of supervision which moves between the client and considering the wider system/organisation impact. Talking Heads was formed in 2018 after a year's support from the School for Social Entrepreneurs. I originally began as a sole trader. I had huge vision and passion but was less sure about running a social enterprise! I began with one Assistant Head in a specialist school and pre-pandemic, asked her to allow me to work with her online to see if I could learn how the relationship could be formed well. Fast forward to 2020 and I am so grateful for the learning. Work and my team have grown entirely by word of mouth. At Talking Heads, we maintain relationships at the core of all work. I have shared our developing model with Education Support which is currently providing the largest scale-up of supervision in education undertaken in the world. I continue to oversee the quality of this work as well as growing Talking Heads. We are a team of 50 and work all over the UK providing robust, long-term supervision to senior leaders and then within the educational setting once senior leaders are fully engaged. We are also developing our training with Penny Sturt to an internal sustainable model, the Integrated Model of Supervision in Schools (IMSS). Senior leaders stay in external supervision as they need it in their role and benefit from it being external.

When I think of all that educators carry, I could not believe that they didn't have supervision. In fact, I thought it was so crazy that I just kept looking around thinking someone else must have done this, or someone else must have noticed. There are supervisors out there who've been working with head teachers/senior leaders. I'm not the first supervisor to work with them, but I guess I'm the first person that's named it in a particular way and upscaled delivery whilst working out how to keep relationships core and not to become simply a brokering service. I know my team well and I personally match and allocate all supervisees with their supervisor at the start. This retains the flexibility to also ask to see someone else if the match is not good.

Lisa C So there's lots that you've mentioned there. I mean, one is around cross-sector working. And that's something I'm very passionate about, largely because children and young people don't tend to operate in a sector. They are exposed, if you like, to lots of different sectors and services. I also like the reflection, "how did I do my best work?" And that really is the essence of this book. How do I do my best work? And what have I seen in my work where that best work is facilitated? I think that leads nicely into thinking about the quality of supervision, because there are sectors where supervision has been highly integrated for a very long time.

If we think about social work, social work long has been engaged in the practice. Yet when I speak to people, whether it is those who give supervision or those who receive supervision, there are often real expressions of disdain. So the supervisor can often feel like they're not trained, they're not qualified, they're simply doing what was done for them. They don't know what the benchmark of good quality ought to be. And for the supervisee, there's often a sense that it's not confidential, it's very case orientated, or that there's no space for reflection.

So in your experience, I guess, first of all, what makes good-quality supervision and what doesn't and what are the implications for an organisation or for a team where good-quality supervision is not in place?

Lisa L-W Good supervision can really go unnoticed, which is why it's quite hard to evidence the outcomes. But you name something key there, about how it is mandated which of course it can be in both health and social care, and whether choice remains about who you work with. People may not attend supervision that does not work for them. Thousands of senior leaders across the UK with Education Support and Talking Heads are attending regular, external, monthly supervision. NInety-nine percent at Education Support have said they would recommend it to a colleague or friend.

I watched a great webinar recently with Robin Shohet and Peter Hawkins talking about spirituality in supervision and Peter said something that named a belief that I have which was around trust and safety. That the supervisee needs to trust the supervisor enough to bring their mistrust. That is key. Essentially supervision is about being able to professionally not know, to be curious about our work and willing to be professionally vulnerable. With this quality of relationship between supervisor and supervisee there is the possibility of being able to be challenged and "comfortable." A sense of relational safety with the supervisor and one where challenge is allowed too, as there is trust that what emerges in supervision will be relevant and delivered/received in a shared place of respect and relationship. This is where regularity of relationship is vital.

Bad supervision is "tick box" and is maybe in place once every few months. Neither supervisor nor supervisee can hold each other in mind or the organisation or any of the threads from the last session. It doesn't happen in the same place. Maybe there's not the same supervisor. It's just a checklist.

Next level of not "good enough" is if the supervisor is trained but the relationship is not a good fit on a human level. I have experienced this several times in my career and is one key problem with mandating supervision and there being no choice about who we share our professional/personal selves with. One of the key processes, especially for external supervision, is the relationship between supervisor and supervisee. Supervision is essentially relational so finding someone a supervisee can work with is key to successful supervision. It is important that when people then come back to me because there is not a good fit, they meet someone else and we can talk about what was not "right" in the relationship. None of us is right for everyone and that includes me. It is important to move on and get it right for the supervisee and therefore the children/young people in their setting.

At Talking Heads all our supervisors are trained and experienced. Supervisors continue to be supervised themselves. The good relationship between supervisor and supervisee allows a range of feelings to come up, including painful ones; a working supervision relationship allows the supervisee to tolerate them arising and know that these feelings are in fact something to do with the work issue they are bringing. Supervision can allow these feelings to be looked at. To allow shared supervision. An objective look at the issue without being overwhelmed by feeling.

A person who has had a bad experience, especially if they are not required by their profession to have supervision, will not be inclined to attend when an offer of good supervision is available. This is of concern as supervision is now becoming known about in education. How do we keep supervision in schools good? How do we ensure the importance of it is understood and those offering it work within the notions of "good" I have outlined?

Good supervision is a place of ethical accountability. Anyone that works with human beings in services wants to do that work for reasons to do with core values and a sense of purpose. It may be less about financial reward.

The higher up you are in an organisation, the more power you have and there may be fewer people who will hold you accountable in an ethical way or challenge you. Supervision is a place that cares about how we're doing something. The senior leaders we work with tell us often how much this matters to them. Establishing a culture from the top and then paying attention to its maintenance is a key factor in the quality of supervision throughout an organisation.

Talking Heads Principles of Good Supervision:

1. A "good" relational fit with trained supervisor in good supervision themselves.
2. Regular—more than a 5/6-week gap means the relationship needs a lot of maintaining each session and this prevents getting to the reflective person/organisational reflective work. In education, three per term works.
3. Planned for in advance and reliable.

Good supervision is also part of continued professional development in that it is developmental and bespoke each month to you and the current context of the children and young people's needs as well as the needs of the organisation and staff team. The supervisee's wellbeing is of key interest in supervision because if we are not feeling ok then we are not able to be our best selves at work or in service of others.

Whether working with a supervisor with a clinical background, social work, education, or other background, what is most important in working with a supervisor you can work with? Do you feel understood by them? Is there the right level of comfort and challenge? Education is in many ways a highly scrutinised profession. Supervision's role fills a gap between external scrutiny and accountability by the likes of Ofsted. It offers a space to recognise the **emotional weight** educators carry in working with children/young people. Particularly as other external support services are diminishing. We need to see more educators training as supervisors but the most important factor in your supervisor is their capacity to not blur boundaries and fall into another role. You need them to be a good supervisor. The only issues I have picked up as we have scaled up have been around supervisors falling into trying to be something other than a supervisor. For example, when we are not experienced enough in a role, e.g. supervisor, and we are inexperienced, then we hear something that appeals to a previous training/role where we feel more confident and experienced and maybe could "rescue" and "help," for example, with a school action plan or something similar, we are no longer being a supervisor. Occasionally, I get pulled into being a therapist. It can still happen and that is one of the many reasons I have supervision. We all get pulled into places! It is hard to recover from this unless the supervisor is in their own supervision and can take what happens in the room to their own supervision. The shift in role will be felt but may not be understood by the supervisee. The supervisor will need help in their own supervision in how to get back into the role with their supervisee.

Lisa C   So you've looked at that balance between challenge and comfort. I'm wondering, is it worth thinking about coaching, mentoring, supervision, and therapy as some sort of Venn diagram with a space in the middle where those different modalities align? For example, that it's all about relationships would live in the middle of that space for me.

It's often a conversation, academically and professionally, regarding what the differences are so if you were to outline the difference, how might you frame that and how might you consider that?

I'm asking that while contemplating that some of the organisations that I work with around culture change really struggle with some of those boundaries where they want to be very trauma informed, very focused on safety, very much focused on the well-being of their staff and their workforce, but then sometimes find themselves in a place where the needs of those using the services become secondary to their own needs as a member of the workforce.

Lisa L-W The whole of a person can come to supervision, but the contract of what supervision is and how it all shows up in the room is attended to for a different reason from counselling and the reason is the beneficiary of service. In this case children/young people.

Even if at times we are deeply embroiled with our supervisees in their well-being and how they are at work, the training, the listening of the supervisor is always ultimately about, can I still hear the client, the beneficiary, the children, here? The supervisor is wondering how what you are sharing is impacting on how you're showing up at work. The boundary is around how to stop that tipping into counselling. There are times where, as a supervisor, something is coming up so often on repeat that you can no longer hear the client.

That would be, as a supervisor, the point at which you would gently but clearly raise "I think this also needs some space somewhere else, as it keeps stopping us being able to hear about the work," and it's amazing when that happens and someone is able to put counselling in place because it frees up all the space again in supervision too, because the pain or issue that is unresolved is being held somewhere else appropriately with a different accountability to take care of the person/supervisee.

Supervision is *always* ultimately about the client and your well-being is key because how you are at work impacts on the people that we work with. But counselling is about you. If you go to counselling and you talk about work, a work issue, the counsellor is going to be interested in how that is impacting on your life, not how is that impacting on the beneficiary. They may help you look backwards, perhaps into family history, with an awareness of some sort of dynamic from childhood, but the counsellor's purpose for hearing about the issue to do with work is to help you live your life going forward.

When we are intentionally working in a trauma-informed way, the demand on the workforce is to be constantly open dynamically to the nonverbal and verbal communications of the children/young people. Nonverbal communication being the most powerful, and this is where understanding of self is key, and supervision helps because otherwise the buildup of being relationally close to trauma of a young person is too much. Ultimately as we know from the likes of van der Kolk and Rothschild, trauma is felt in the body, held in the body. It is also the case that many of us who do this work do so because we are in some ways in territory of our own pain, and we choose to work in helping fields where we deeply wish things to be somehow different than they were for us.

Lisa C I think that's a beautiful distinction, clear, concise, and I can see so clearly where if that is not held by a suitably experienced and qualified supervisor, that can get very tricky. Because of course we bring ourselves to work. Of course we want to know why something is pushing my buttons and why is this response happening for me.

Lisa L-W Unpicking that can fall into either camp of counselling or supervision but the reason to do it in supervision is because we need to understand what is happening to us so we can work with a child around it safely. The thing that keeps it safe is being clear that the reason to unpick it together is to help understand what is going on at work and improve outcomes for children and young people. The main way of healing trauma is in a healthy relationship with a kind, consistent and empathic other/s. Without supervision in place the internal capacity of adults becomes reduced. They are only human. We are human, and we get full from our lives outside work as well as inside work. We need help to off-load and make sense of what is going on when doing such deep work. And the circle of support must be in place. The supervisor needs to be in good supervision themselves.

Lisa C The anchor is so clear; it is the beneficiary, the client, the baby, the child, the young person.

Y6 Teacher in mainstream Primary—near retirement and known for being warm hearted, loving her job and having never been off sick. Young person in class who is in foster care but moving into an adoptive relationship with current foster family. The child becomes increasingly distressed as adoption approaches.

I am asked to offer short-term support. We have six sessions.

In the first three sessions all the feelings are named whilst making sure a relationship is built. Fortunately, we have worked alongside each other before so a good and trusting relationship is present. The teacher names experiencing stress, lack of sleep, anger, disgust at her own feelings, feeling out of control, frightened, unsafe, and worthless. All these feelings were a surprise and made her feel ashamed. At a particular point, when there was a pause for breath and the timing felt right, I was able to ask a question around how the teacher thought the young person was feeling about their life. She paused and had a profound insight and acknowledgement that the feelings named previously, which she had described as her own, did in fact belong to the young person. This is not a conscious process of transferring feelings but an unconscious one. Without intervention this teacher would have gone off sick and, worst of all, would have come to believe these experiences as true about who she now was as a teacher. Instead her distance and compassion were restored.

Supervision helped her see that these feelings belonged to the young person and that they needed an adult to understand, name, and contain relationally and robustly in a way that meant their feelings were not doing the adult harm.

Lisa L-W Holding on to that anchor is how supervision helps to keep practice safe and boundaried. It involves meeting people at their edges: accountability, risk, competency, fitness to practise. Safeguarding. It also has a huge role to play in reminding supervisees about what we all forget which is to take care of our bodies and to make sure we complete the stress cycle (Nagoski & Nagoski, 2019) by exercising in ways that complete the stress response. They refer to the importance of moving, physical contact that is soothing for at least 20 seconds with someone we have a good relationship with, and they remind us to sleep. These three factors will mean we reduce our stress hormones. We literally need to excrete through our skin our buildup of stress! I have often reminded supervisees that if this also brings them joy that is extra positive so dancing in your kitchen is fine if it also elevates your heart rate!

Lisa C We've looked at the difference between supervision and counselling. Can you briefly also make the distinction around coaching and mentoring?

Lisa L-W Coaching has become well established in education and it is interesting that it has arrived first in one way but makes complete sense when we think about it from the point of view that coaching matches education culturally. It is short term, focused on the professional, and goal oriented. It may focus on role, but its remit is not the children/young people or about safeguarding, ethical accountability in role, and impact on the setting/children. It works well alongside supervision and if you experience both you will feel how different they are in purpose.

Mentoring similarly focuses on role and its development and may well, like coaching, pay attention to well-being but it is often connected to line management processes and career progression. It is about the mentee and not fundamentally connected to the relationship between mentee and beneficiary. It is about performance. It has judgement within it. It is not about emotional labour.

Lisa C So how does supervision support cultures in settings to develop so that trauma-informed practice can exist without fear of burnout of staff?

Which I guess that links to the last question that I raised, which is that when you are trying to create trauma-informed cultures, there is a cost that is different on the person.

Lisa L-W Absolutely. Where you've got a staff team in a trauma-informed education setting where staff are emotionally regulated, and, therefore, we can imagine has educators with an internal capacity for connection, then the young person can safely project onto them what the child needs to know in themselves; as we saw in the case study previously, that all impacts on culture. It is individuals that make up a culture, but it is how we are interdependent and impact on each other which creates how the culture feels. Working in a well-supported trauma-informed setting is an amazing experience. It is a brave place of safety and resilience. One of confidence and where risks can also be taken by staff and children and young people because the culture is dynamic, reflective, and responsive. Also, creative! These kinds of cultures rarely see staff burnout. Burnout can happen in any profession but as Lisa Nel affirms in her work, vicarious trauma is a real risk to teachers who engage in a whole human way with traumatised children. It can impact their worldview if the buildup of distress they accept in their bodies is not acknowledged and discharged both emotionally and physically. As Lisa says, you cannot get in the water and not get wet!

It is often at a senior leader level that you're going to hear more about the culture in supervision and that's what you're going to be supervising, or interpersonal relationships that are playing out and have needed to come to supervision. You will often be going between the relational in a team and then looking at the wider system, which also includes the wider picture, the world; you know, recent elections in this country and across the world have been having an impact. Senior leaders engaging in supervision are having a regular opportunity to off-load and reflect on all they need to bring to a session. It helps them, as one of my supervisees describes it, keep swimming and loving it! It helps them stay fit and healthy and not be exhausted. Everyone looks to the senior leaders to see what both is said and importantly what cannot be said or done. In trauma-informed settings where senior leaders are in supervision regularly and take time to attend, the impact is experienced by all those in relationship with them. We hear our supervisees make jokes about how partners or close colleagues will check in on when the next supervision is as they have noticed their colleague is stressed. It means they have noticed the impact of supervision previously too. The senior leader is modelling in a real way that professional vulnerability is valued. That reflection is valued and therefore also that curiosity about our work and safely not knowing and asking questions is ok. We have repeated feedback from the trauma-informed settings we work with that supervision—where all senior leadership are in supervision and maybe also pastoral teams—that the quality of conversations about children and the level and style of challenge is braver, more challenging, and done with a confidence and security that rarely happens when teams are not in supervision.

What happens in our wider system—COVID, racist riots, war—those are all impactful. Schools are microcosms of all the bigger issues that are playing out in our society and somehow heads in schools are expected to contain all this tension.

Lisa C So that leads me nicely into thinking about the role of supervision and anti-racist practice. And I am so pleased that you've brought up the summer riots, for example, because they happened during a period where schools were closed, and I think there must have been all sorts of concerns about how schools were going to receive children back in September. I imagined consideration being given to how they were going to name it to tame it, to coin Dan Seigel's phrase, and how might they express it to address it, to take Cathy Malchiodi's phrase. In other words, I imagined that they would be thinking long and hard about how they were going to find ways to hold all the potentially different narratives of the families and children that were going to come back into that school.

I surmised that there were would be a spectrum ranging from, it didn't affect us, pretending it didn't happen, right the way through to it completely enveloping everything. In your experience, what did you find came up? How did supervision support the workforce in that context? And what are the wider implications for thinking about anti-racism and managing it and Islamophobia in education settings?

Lisa L-W That's a lot of questions. I did a lot of thinking, feeling over the summer about how people would return in autumn 2024, and I did a lot of thinking collectively with my team to ensure that we were prepared to meet distress. What we have found as a team, seeing hundreds of senior leaders over the UK, is that many people have been putting blinkers on. Systemically people have—leaders have—felt overwhelmed and that they can't deal with the enormity of global issues that presently exist and a mindset of "I'm just going to focus on all of the crises and complexities I need to try and manage in my own school."

The practical use of blinkers on a cart horse is that they are there so the horse is not distracted or frightened by anything and can keep to its task of going forward.

This has been the message since the move out of the pandemic combined with a move to the right politically alongside a decline in economic stability. Shohet and Hawkins again talk about how organisations that exist to help others will reflect unresolved societal issues and mode 7 of their supervision model trains us to pay attention to this wider context.

We need to be aware of the culture of our school, our workplace, our classroom, our staffrooms so that microaggressions as well as more obvious attacks on these protected characteristics can be challenged.

Relationship is key to the capacity to undertake this kind of work so that shame does not arise, and it is finely balanced and skilful. If we tip our supervisees into shame, they are unlikely, without a good relationship, to be able to tolerate naming these struggles or to receive challenge around racism, for example. They will dysregulate and hide themselves in future. But this work is vital to all our work with humans but particularly so in settings which are supporting those who have been let down by the system and where other humans/adults did not adequately care for them and who have been abused. Abuse happens within relationships where there is a power imbalance. Schools hold many versions of this all the time. It is not possible ethically to undertake the work without good supervision in place and supervisors need to remain alert to recognising vicarious trauma where supervisees may become vulnerable over time by being consistently open to the wounds of others.

Lisa C I was also thinking about anti-racist practice and the rise in Islamophobia, and I think you've described there how challenging it can be to bring that to the fore, while also acknowledging that for many schools and communities, it's at the fore all the time.

Lisa L-W The complexities of human differences and similarities that schools hold is one of the reasons, again, that I wanted to bring supervision in, because holding this level of external conflict that gets played out among primary school children, secondary school children, teachers, parents, and local communities is profound.

It was more alarming before the general election in this country. The rise in schools, even down here in Devon, of more right-wing conversations that were happening and being played out in primary schools was scary and had become normalised.

We are working with people that are coming from different ends in a spectrum of beliefs and political views, and we supervise a full range of people, and that's also a live learning conversation. Differences of political, religious beliefs exist between supervisee and supervisor, and it is here in a good relationship that risks can be taken and blinkers identified but potentially safely challenged and, some, removed when the time is right. Supervision, I believe, should play an active role in bringing oppression and racism that shows up in sessions into the light so it can be looked at, together.

Lisa C This mirrors the experience of a leader, of somebody leading a team or leading a school setting, which speaks to *all* that complexity and all of the different ways of viewing the world, with different perspectives and different lenses. If we are entirely engaged in the wellbeing of the workforce and caring for the people who care, then belonging, equity, and inclusion have to be a priority regardless of how that is perceived.

Reflection

Effective supervision must consider broader systemic and cultural issues, including the impact of societal events and the need for anti-racist practices. This ensures that the supervision process is relevant and responsive to the complex realities faced by professionals. Lisa Lea Weston offers a compelling argument for the central importance of supervision that not only focuses on our care but centrally locates the care of those whom we walk alongside in the work we do.

The critical role of supervision in professional settings and the need for a comprehensive, supportive, and culturally aware approach is vital to ensure the well-being of both professionals and the clients they serve.

Discussion Points

1. **Recognising the Impact of Bad Supervision**
   - Have I ever experienced supervision that felt critical or undermining? How did it affect my confidence and professional growth?
   - How can I help rebuild trust in supervision for staff who have had previous negative experiences?
2. **Defining the Qualities of Good Supervision**
   - What makes supervision feel safe, supportive, and developmental for me or my team?
   - How regularly and consistently do I engage in supervision, and is the fit between supervisor and supervisee effective?

3. **Clarifying the Supervisor's Role**
   - How do I balance supporting the emotional well-being of staff while maintaining a clear focus on outcomes for children, families, or service users?
   - Am I aware of the boundary between supervision and counselling, and how do I manage this in practice?
4. **High-Quality Support**
   - What does an effective supervision relationship look like, and how can I help nurture one that allows for both challenge and support?
   - When personal issues arise repeatedly in supervision, how do I decide whether a referral to counselling is appropriate?
5. **Addressing Systemic and Cultural Contexts**
   - How do wider societal issues—such as racism, Islamophobia, or inequality—affect the staff and clients I work with?
   - In what ways does my supervision practice acknowledge and address systemic oppression or organisational culture?
6. **Embedding Anti-Racist and Inclusive Practice**
   - Do I create space in supervision to talk about identity, race, religion, or cultural bias when they impact practice?
   - How do I support my team in recognising and challenging racism and other forms of discrimination in the workplace?
7. **Building Trauma-Informed Supervision Structures**
   - Do I approach supervision with an understanding that many staff are holding vicarious or lived trauma?
   - How do I maintain a trauma-informed approach that supports regulation, reflection, and resilience?

8. **Leadership and Organisational Responsibility**
   - What role do I play in ensuring supervision contributes to a culture of psychological safety and emotional wellbeing across my team or organisation?
   - How can leaders model and prioritise trauma-informed, reflective supervision that values both professional growth and personal support?

References

BACP. *Supervision Resources Ethical Framework for the Counselling Professions*. https://www.bacp.co.uk/events-and-resources/ethics-and-standards/ethical-framework-for-the-counselling-professions/supervision/, accessed on 20th March 2025.

Education Support. *Wellbeing Support for School and FE Leaders*. https://www.educationsupport.org.uk/get-help/help-for-your-staff/wellbeing-services/professional-supervision/, accessed on 20th March 2025.

Nagoski, E., & Nagoski, A. (2019). *Burnout: The Secret to Unlocking the Stress Cycle*. Ballantine Books.

Epilogue

I started this book from a place of exploration about what it takes to "do the work" from a place of learning to live with an uncurable but treatable cancer. It feels a little ironic to now be at the end of this book having just been told that the cancer has returned already, just eight months after a stem cell transplant. The average remission is 5 to 10 years so I feel a little cheated, if feeling cheated is allowed when we are blessed to have so many treatment options. Multiple myeloma is not a million miles away from having been a death sentence. I think I will afford myself the luxury of feeling grateful and cheated all at once.

*

Every conversation in this book has so much to teach us. The simple conversation style might suggest a simplicity of thought and a way of thinking that can often be attributed to "common sense." However, be under no illusion; the practice experience, the lived experiences, and the academic research and theory that underpins every one of these conversations must not be underestimated. It is extensive and runs into decades of learning.

The learning opportunity provided is designed for you to action, to make changes, to create something better than you have experienced before. This action is ultimately about what you now do for yourself, how you will feel about and understand your colleagues and, where you are able, create systemic changes for all. In doing so, what can be delivered in our work will become exemplary.

May we move gracefully onwards: driven, hopeful, and prepared!

Further Reading

Ali, H. (2021a). 'Don't speak for us': How mainstream media misrepresents Muslim women. *The New Arab*. https://www.newarab.com/features/how-mainstream-media-misrepresents-muslim-women, accessed on 16th March 2025.

Ali, H. (2021b). Exclusion on the frontline: The discrimination, racism and Islamophobia impacting Muslim healthcare professionals. *The New Arab*. https://www.newarab.com/features/discrimination-faced-uks-muslim-healthcare-workers, accessed on 16th March 2025.

Ali, H. (2022). How leaders can better support Muslim women at work. *Harvard Business Review*. https://hbr.org/2022/07/how-leaders-can-better-support-muslim-women-at-work, accessed on 16th March 2025.

Ali, H. (2023). Why I had an arranged marriage—and it doesn't make me any less progressive. *The Independent*. https://www.independent.co.uk/voices/arranged-marriage-jemima-goldsmith-age-b2290539.html, accessed on 16th March 2025.

Ali, H. (2024). No school—not even Britain's 'strictest headteacher', Katharine Birbalsingh—should have the Right to Ban Prayer. *The Independent*. https://www.independent.co.uk/voices/katharine-birbalsingh-strictest-head teacher-ban-prayer-muslim-b2529695.html, accessed on 16th March 2025.

Atlas, G. (2022). *Emotional Inheritance: A Therapist, Her Patients, and the Legacy of Trauma*. Little, Brown Spark.

BACP. *Supervision Resources Ethical Framework for the Counselling Professions*. https://www.bacp.co.uk/events-and-resources/ethics-and-standards/ethical-framework-for-the-counselling-professions/supervision/, accessed on 20th March 2025.

Blackie, S. (2023). *Hagitude: Reimagining the Second Half of Life*. Duckworth Books.

Bomber, L., Golding, K., & Sian Phillips, S. (2020). *Working with Relational Trauma in Schools: An Educator's Guide to Using Dyadic Developmental Practice*. Jessica Kingsley Publishers.

Further Reading

Brave Heart, M. Y. H. (2003). The historical trauma response among natives and its relationship with substance abuse: A Lakota illustration. *Journal of Psychoactive Drugs*, 35(1), 7–13.

Brierley, A. (2019). *Your Honour Can I Tell You My Story?* Waterside Press.

Brooks, R. (2019). *The Trauma and Attachment-Aware Classroom: A Practical Guide to Supporting Children Who Have Encountered Trauma and Adverse Childhood Experiences*. Jessica Kingsley Publishers.

Chesner, A., & Lykou, S. (2021). *Trauma in the Creative and Embodied Therapies. When Words are Not Enough*. Oxon: Routledge.

Codrington, K. (2022). *Second Spring*. HarperCollins Publishers.

Danieli, Y. (Ed.). (1998). *International Handbook of Multigenerational Legacies of Trauma*. Springer.

Desautels, L. (2024). *Connections Over Compliance: Rewiring Our Perceptions of Discipline*. Wyatt-MacKenzie Publishing.

Dix, P. (2021). *After the Adults Change. Achievable Behaviour Nirvana*. Independent Thinking Press.

Dokter, D., Lea-Weston, L., & Thornewood, T. (2023). Waving and drowning: The gradations of therapist fitness to practise. *Dramatherapy*, 44(1), 7–17.

Education Support. *Wellbeing Support for School and FE Leaders*. https://www.educationsupport.org.uk/get-help/help-for-your-staff/wellbeing-services/professional-supervision/, accessed on 20th March 2025.

Finnis, M. (2021). *Restorative Practice. Building Relationships, Improving Behaviour and Creating Stronger Communities*. Independent Thinking Press.

Graham, H., & McNeill, F. (2017). Desistance: Envisioning futures. In Carlen, P., & Ayres França, L. (eds.) *Alternative Criminologies* (pages 433–451). London: Routledge.

Hawkins, P., & Shohet, R. (2012). *Supervision in the Helping Professions*. Berkshire: Open University Press.

Hübl, T., & Avritt, J. J. (2020). *Healing Collective Trauma: A Process for Integrating Our Intergenerational and Cultural Wounds*. Sounds True.

Innes-Turnill, D. (2025). *Safeguarding in the Classroom*. London: Sage.

Jude, N., Moore, T., & Simango, G. (2025). *The Anti-Racist Social Worker in Practice*. Routledge.

Levine, P. A. (1997). *Waking the Tiger: Healing Trauma*. Berkeley: North Atlantic Books.

Menakem, R. (2017). *My Grandmother's Hands: Racialized Trauma and the Pathway to Mending Our Hearts and Bodies*. Central Recovery Press.

Mucci, C. (2013). *Beyond Individual and Collective Trauma: Intergenerational Transmission, Psychoanalytic Treatment, and the Dynamics of Forgiveness*. Karnac Books.

Further Reading

Nagoski, E., & Nagoski, A. (2019). *Burnout: The Secret to Unlocking the Stress Cycle*. Ballantine Books.

Plumbly, C. (2024). *Burnout: How to Manage Your Nervous System Before it Manages You*. Hodder & Stoughton.

Pope, A., & Wurlitzer, S. H. (2022). *Wise Power*. Hay House.

Rothschild, B. (2010). *8 Keys to Safe Trauma Recovery*. London: W.W. Norton & Company.

Shaffi, S. (2022). Five Muslim women on why they love Ms. Marvel and their hopes for the Disney+ show. *The New Arab*. https://www.newarab.com/features/five-muslim-women-why-they-love-ms-marvel, accessed on 16th March 2025.

Sotero, M. M. (2006). A conceptual model of historical trauma: Implications for public health practice and research. *Journal of Health Disparities Research and Practice*, 1(1), 93–108.

Sturt, P., & Rowe, J. (2023). *Using Supervision in Schools*. Shoreham by Sea: Pavilion Publishing and Media Ltd.

Supervision as Spiritual Practice Workshop. https://onlinevents.co.uk/courses/supervision-as-spiritual-practice-workshop-with-peter-hawkins-robin-shohet/.

Treisman, K. (2024). *Trauma Deck of Cards*. Jessica Kingsley Publishers.

Wolynn, M. (2016). *It Didn't Start with You: How Inherited Family Trauma Shapes Who We Are and How to End the Cycle*. Penguin Books.

Yehuda, R., & Lehrner, A. (2018). Intergenerational transmission of trauma effects: Putative role of epigenetic mechanisms. *World Psychiatry*, 17(3), 243–257.

Index

acceptance, change (requirement) 37
ACE study (Felitti) 185
action plans: development 82; fairness/inclusiveness 83
activation, occurrence 140–141
activist burnout, workshops/training 143
addiction: consideration 178; importance, belief 184; trauma, separation 178
admin work: avoidance 47–48; teacher avoidance 47–48
Adoption Consultancy 360, The 223
adultification: bias 96; impact 96; issues 81
adults, internal capacity (reduction) 232
Adverse Childhood Experiences (ACEs): coordinated work 11; serious violence, link 12
adversity 12, 213; embedding 16; experiences 165; impact 22; lived experiences 162; lived experiences, harnessing 163
Adversity Trauma and Resilience (ATR) agenda, advancing 14
Adversity Trauma and Resilience (ATR) Programme 8–9, 11; birth 11–13; methodology, testing

23; resources/funding, limitation (frustration) 16
advocates, coalition (building) 14
agency costs, payment 61
Ai, Hira (conversation) 101
alcohol care teams, development 9
alcoholism, treatment 178–179
alien cultures, perspective 89
allyship: anti-racist allyship, practice 128; consideration 147; fostering 111–112; importance 77; Prophet Muhammad exemplification 111; support 102
ancestral trauma 77, 138, 148–150; awareness, absence 151
annual leave, agreement (need) 69
anti-Muslim sentiment, manifestation 113
anti-racism: awareness 128–129; consideration 147
anti-racist allyship, practice 127
anti-racist discussion, joining/ engagement 95–96
anti-racist local authority, becoming 86
anti-racist practice 79–80; considerations 94, 238–239; embedding, difficulty 92–93; ongoing learning, impact 82; work, imperfections 88

247

Index

anti-racist project board, existence 84
anti-racist strategic action planning: aim 80; implications/need 78
anti-racist strategies, development 82
anti-racist training 131–132; delivery 81
anxiety, increase 76
apartheid 149
APM (company operation) 27
appointments, making 49
arranged marriages, misunderstanding 110
articulation, enjoyment 208
ASDA, lifestyle (relationship) 46
Asian communities (trauma), racist ideology (impact) 89
asylum seekers, interaction 78–79
Atkins, William 51
attendance, data entry 47–48
autonomic nervous system (ANS) 4, 199
awareness-raising 131; impact 18–19

balance, consideration 33–34
Baldwin, James 142
BASW World Social Work Day 81
behaviour, individual aspects (ignoring) 132
beliefs, reflection 94
Belly of the Whale, archetype 192
belonging: considerations 75; human motivational need 77; power, feeling 75–76; sense, impacts 89; sense, providing 85–86
BGM communities, questions 90–91
BGM social workers, support (providing) 90

BGM staff members, racial trauma (impact) 84
BGM workforce, needs (listening) 86
biases: adultification bias 96; lens 88; reflections 94; workforce learning 80
Bible, misinterpretations 112
binary personal/professional sef 63
binary thinking, impact 120
birth-assigned gender 196
Black adults, behaviour (concern) 87
Black children, behaviour (concern) 87
Black children/families, racial trauma (impact) 81
Black communities: engagement, ease 90–91; racial trauma 91–92; targeting, ethnicity/faith weaponisation 104; trauma, racist ideology (impact) 89
Black fathers: interaction 81, 96; stereotypes 96
Black history, erasure (attempts) 93
Black History Month 97
Blackie, Sharon 200
Black psychotherapist, impact 86
Black staff members: fears, considerations 92; social events/bring and share events, organisation 97; support/opportunities, improvement 80–81
blinkers, use 237–238
body (bodies): awareness 3–4; biological hierarchies 210
boundaries: compassion 18; role-modelling, importance 15
brain, biological hierarchies 210

Index

Brayne, Mark 185
Brighton growth community 88
Brighton & Hove City Council, strategic anti-racist lead employment 79
Brown communities, targeting (ethnicity/faith weaponisation) 104
Brunt, Amelia (conversation) 196
budgets, writing (need) 69
burnout 6, 203, 214; menopausal burnout 214; occurrence 235; prevention 47; risk/vulnerability 213; susceptibility 214
Burnout Inventory (Maslach) 203

Campbell-Stephens, Rosemary 94
capitalism: impact 93; racial formation/colonialism, impact 134
care: need 42–43; over-prioritising, possibility 33; structure support 18
career progression 234
care experience 56–57; focus 66–67
care-experienced person, sharing 63
caregiver, need 185–186
caring, costs 143
CBT (online courses) 60–61
central nervous system, tuning in 3
chair of the board, behaviour 58–59
change: cultivation 20; driving 21–24
Cherry, Lisa 143
chicken pox (school attendance) 53–54
chief executive, behaviour 58–59
Child and Adolescent Mental Health Team (CAMHS) 169–170
childhood: adversity 164; experiences, impact 40; foundation 52–53; learning 173; poverty of circumstance, presence 53
children: anger 87; cultural identity/religion/belonging, enhancement 88–89; force-feeding 222; outcomes, improvement 232; safeguarding 78–79; self-awareness 165; tying 222
Children and Family Court Advisory and Support Service (Cafcass), family support 57
children/families, social work 57
child sexual exploitation/abuse, usage 103
child trafficking, social work 79
CIC Wellbeing 32–33
CIPD survey 204
classism: presence 186; racial formation/colonialism, impact 134
class, race (intersection) 134
classroom assistant role 30
client, supervision (relationship) 231
climate change, awareness 201
Climbié, Victoria (murder) 129
clinical hypnosis, training 178
clinicians, education 188
coaching: capability stage 51; discussion 229; importance 50, 234; relationships, focus 214; sharing 145; work 212–213
coach, need 51
collaboration, usage 16
collaborative system-wide approach, power (demonstration) 20
collective care, consideration 5

249

Index

collective trauma 138
colonialism 118; impact 93, 134; power 94–95
colonial legacy, influence 118
colonisation: aspects 118; consideration 139; impact 93
commitment, result 31–32
communication: improvement 144–145; patterns 150–151; skills 29–30
communities: power 155; resourcing 155; thriving 167
communities of practice, presence 131
Community Care Live 81
compassion: excess, impossibility 17; importance 17–18
compassionate fatigue, workshops/training 143
competency: importance 51; job description, alignment 44
confidence 36
confidentiality 222
connection, internal capacity 235
conversations, infusion 145
co-regulating caregiver, reliance 185
co-regulation: experiences 186; usage 4
cost of living, expense rates (relationship) 62
counseling 232; offer 61; provision 60
COVID-19: impact 63, 236; media bias 106
CPD course 42–43
creative expression 155
creativity 155; increase 119, 132
Credit Union, The 48
criminal justice 12

criminal justice system: lived experiences 27, 31, 35; lived experiences, absence 34
crisis, children/families experience 58–69
critical whiteness studies 118–119
Croft, Darren 212
cross-sectionality 197
cultural affinity groups, example 142–143
cultural awareness, building 109
cultural genogram, usage 148–149
cultural identity 76
cultural literacy, fostering 111–112
cultural needs 120
cultural norms, understanding 80–81
cultural shift, fostering 15
culture: change, need 68; education 113; supervision support 234
cyclical predictability, loss 205
cyclicity, awareness 208

daily interactions, impact 18
danger, detection 4
Dante's Inferno 192
decolonisation, discussion (responses) 121
decolonising: practice 77; process 118; trauma, relationship 119–120
Deconstructing the Anti-Racist Ally (Hinchliffe) 127
Delap, Gaie 201
Deliveroo 50–51
depersonalisation 203
depressive symptoms 76
desistance terms 29
developmental trauma 185

250

Index

director of children's services, behaviour 58–59
disability 76
disciplinarian approaches, impact 122
discomfort, feeling 152
disconnection 191
discrimination 93; staff lived experiences 82–83; systemic discrimination, display 123–124; theme 148–149
disease model, entrenchment 183–184
displacement, consideration 139
diverse leaders programme, development 84
diversity, equality, and inclusion (DEI): initiatives, consideration/preparation 97; lens 93; strategies 79; tick box exercise 85
diversity of thought, increase 132
Dokter, Ditty 223
domestic abuse, experience 63
drama therapy 202
drop-in sessions, setup 95–96
dysregulation 168, 188; somatic dysregulation 182

early life: attachment, experiences 199; trauma 212–213
education: importance, parent perspective 53–54; leadership, love (display) 40; system, discussion 44; usage 18–19
educational leadership, mastery 46–47
educators: emotional weight 229; lived experiences, harnessing 163; well-being 221

embodied wisdom 151
emotional dysregulation 185–186
emotional expression, relationship 140
emotional heavy lifting 142
emotional labour, usage 127
emotional system, support/buffering 147
emotional weight 229
empathy: perfect storm 206; result 31–32, 171–172
empire, power 94–95
employee assistance programmes, counseling (provision) 60
employee care, trauma-informed approach 31
epigenetics 151
equality, diversity, and inclusion (EDI) agenda 127
ethnicity, irrelevance 104
Eurocentric lens, usage 80–81
"Evolution of the Adversity, Trauma, and Resilience Programme: A Journey Towards a Trauma-Informed System" (discussion) 8
exclusion system, impact 75
exhaustion, prevention 47
expense rates, cost of living (relationship) 62
expenses, signing (need) 69
experience, usage (value) 66
expression, freedom 103
eye, movement desensitisation and reprocessing (EMDR) 185

face-to-face therapy, usage 61
faith, avoidance 107
faith-based stereotyping, avoidance 108

251

Index

famine 148
far right ideology, description 103
far-right narratives, impact 104
fascism 89
fatigue, perfect storm 206
Fawcett Society 204
fears 191; consideration 92
feedback: acceptance 124; repetition 236
FGM/C services 79
financial support, loss 155
fitness, loss 51
Floyd, George (murder): injustice 95; witnessing 91
forced displacement 148
forgiveness 153–154
friendliness, love 47
frustration, feeling 152
future, consideration 191

Gacaca Courts 154
Gaza: genocides/persecution, collective trauma 110; US ownership, Trump statement 101
gender: diversity 76, 197; systemic irregularities 213
genocides 145, 153; collective trauma 110; experiences 153, 156; Rwandan genocide 148; suffering 153
genogram 149; cultural genogram 148–149
global issues, enormity 237
Global Majority: definition 94; people, disadvantages 126–127
goals, shared understanding 12
Good Ally, The (Reid) 97
good Muslims/bad Muslims, dichotomy (narrative) 106–107

governance: exercise, need 69; impact 59
grooming gangs, prosecution 104
groups, underrepresentation/ overrepresentation 84–85
guilt, feeling 152

harm (addition), chance (reduction) 144
hate, eradication 95
Hawkins, Peter 226, 238
headship, nightmare 43
healing: circles, example 143; journey 188–189; personal healing journey, importance 188; practices/routines/rituals 151–152; relationality 153–154; role 177; space, opening 144
health: crisis, term (observation) 201; inequalities 19; problems, experiencing 63
health/care: sectors 12; system, priorities 9–10
health-harming behaviours 10
heart: hurt 52; pain/scarring 51
helping professions 56
Her Majesty's Inspector of Children's Social Care, work 57
Hero's Journey, archetype 192
Her Way to the Top (Ali) 102
hijab: bias, vocalness 103; media bias 106; wearing, individual preference 107; wearing, meaning 150
Hinchliffe, Jane (conversation) 117
historical injustices 145
historical trauma 93, 140
history, erasure/revision 150–151
HIV, contracting 155

Index

HIV services 79
Holocaust 148–149
homeostasis, maintenance 199, 209
homophobia, presence 186
homophobic environments, impact 76
hooks, bell 130
Hospicing Modernity (Oliveira) 123
hospitals, tobacco control 9
"How to Support Muslim Women" (Cherry) 103
Hugo-Wurlitzer, Sjanie 200
human connectedness, importance 76
human cost, understanding 22
human differences/similarities, complexities 239
human interaction, importance 60
humanity: assistance 49; handling 51
hurt, impact 154–155
hyper-vigilance 4

identity: change, requirement 37; shaping 189
immobilised state 4
imperialist white supremacist capitalist patriarchy 130
Improving Population Health Programme (IPHP): evolution 9; VRP partnership, formation 11
inclusivity, importance 108–109
indigenous knowledge/practices, positioning (issues) 151–152
indigenous wisdom 120
individuality, allowance 172
individuals, re-traumatisation 12
individual trauma 138
inequality system, impact 75
inequity, eradication 95
information technology (IT) savviness 30
Ingeus Academy 28–29; building 30; employees, welfare 31; ensuring 31
Ingeus Justice team: interaction 28–29; joining, induction (attendance) 34
Ingeus UK: Director of Justice services role 28; services delivery 27
Ingeus workforce, entry 30
inherited trauma, awareness (absence) 151
injustice: challenge 95; eradication 95
inner-city school, leading 40
Inner London Education Authority (ILEA), uniform (wearing) 53
Innes-Turnill, Debbie 220
institutional neglect 76
Integrated Care Board (ICB): Leadership, trauma-informed perspective 14; plan, trauma/adversity (embedding) 16; transition 8–9
Integrated Care System (ICS), joining 8–9
Integrated Model of Supervision in Schools (IMSS) 224
intergenerational connection 152
intergenerational healing 152
intergenerational historical trauma 93
intergenerational trauma 77, 93, 138–140, 142, 145; awareness, absence 151; field, communication patterns 150–151; highlighting 156; impact 152
intergenerational wisdom 152

Index

International Women's Day 97
interoception 209; importance 208
interpersonal anti-racism 123–124
Interpersonal Neurobiology (Siegel) 207
interpersonal racism: focus 132; reduction 124
intersectional approach 119
Irving, Emmerline (conversation) 8
Islam: employee education 109; marriages, topic (misunderstanding/misrepresentation) 112
Islamophobia: addressing 101, 147; fueling 105; impact 77; impact, understanding 111; misunderstandings 111; organisational misunderstandings 109–110; pervasiveness, witnessing 102–103; recognition 101, 102; rise 238–239; understanding/addressing, organizational commitment 113

jellyfish zap moment 146
Jewish community, upsetting (fear) 133–134
Johari window *125*, 125–126

Kemp, Alexander (conversation) 56
Kerr, Millie (conversation) 78
keynote presentations, delivery 81
Kgotia 154
King Charles III, Commonwealth head (perceptions) 95
Kinship team 223
knowledge: exchange event, hosting 12–13; level, body reflection 50–51

Layman's Guide to Psychiatry and Psychoanalysis, A (Berne) 178
leaders: articulation 45; behaviour 59; characteristics 67; description 67–68; diverse leaders programme, development 84; experience 239; function 59; influence 59; reflective reading groups, occurrence 96–97; support 143–144; support offering 61–62
leadership: absence 19; actions 69; approach 13; collaboration 19; dislike, impact 45; examination 5; focus 67, 214; management, distinction 67; mastery, display 46; menopause, connection 200; operation 69; positions 45; quality 45; request 49; requirement 68; role 20–21; simplicity 69; space, working 40; work, differences 7
leadership buy-in: achievement 13–14; placement 19; securing 18–19
learning: impact 122; journey 162; personal responsibility 126
Lebentz, Lou (conversation) 177
Levine, Peter 207
LGBT+ homelessness, charity work 57
life, leading 34
lifestyle, interaction 46
line management processes 234
line managers, supervision 32–33
Listening Project, The 21–24
listening skills 29–30
lived experiences 27, 164; employment 31–32; overidentification, absence 36;

shared lived experience, absence (feeling) 34; usage, willingness 35–36
local authorities (sectors) 12
long-term desistance 37
long-term psychological effects 76
love: importance 41–42; need 42–43; personal cost 43; thriving 41; work of love, performing 43
lunch breaks 33

Malchiodi, Cathy 237
management: leadership, relationship 67; task, absence 67
managers: criticism/shaming, impact 141; description 67–68; experience 78; operation, ability 69; support 143–144
marginalised communities (trauma), racist ideology (impact) 89
marketing ploy 191–192
Mato Output 154
mattering: exploration 75; importance 76
Me and My White Supremacy (Saad) 97; white senior leaders/staff reading 83
media bias 105–106
media role, challenge 107
medical trauma 146
mediocrity, nonacceptance 43–44
menopausal burnout 214
menopause: burnout 206; evolutionary edge 211–212; experience 196–197; impact 199–200; medical definition 205–206; perimenopause 205; physical symptoms 213; psychological processes, awareness 201–202; self-leadership/leadership, connection 200; strengths-based examination 196; symptoms 200–201; transition, experience 204
menopausing workforce, skillsets (retention) 204
Menstrual Cycle Awareness and Conscious Menopause (study) 202
menstrual cycle, emotional landscape (tracking) 207
mental exhaustion, perfect storm 206
mental health: impact, ignoring 87; research 203–204; struggles 192
mental health in schools team (MHST) 169
mentoring: discussion 229; focus 234; sharing 145
mentorship, focus 214
microaggressions 76, 238; meaning 123–124; racial microaggression, identification/understanding 124
micro-dosing, usage 145
migration, theme 148–149
mind-body connection 182
mind, expansion 187
minimum wage 42
misgendering 126
mistakes, making 41
mobilised state 4
momentum, loss 19
money, discussion (avoidance) 49
moral conviction, example 104
moral distress, occurrence 6
moral injury 6; workshops/training 143
motivations: importance 45; young people, impact 51–52

Index

motives, alignment 44
Multi Academy Trust (MAT) 50, 52
multi-agency partnerships 96
multigenerational trauma 140
music (making), love (absence) 41
Muslim men: events, attendance (comfort) 108; narrative normalisation, child sexual exploitation/abuse (usage) 103
Muslims: authentic stories/lived experiences, sharing 114; collective blame 110; communities, racial trauma 91; culture, misunderstandings 111; inclusive environment, creation 108; marriages, social responsibility 112; negative perceptions 108; psychological safety, importance 109–110
Muslim women: alienness/incompatibility, perception 106; events, attendance (comfort) 108; image, distortion 113; individuality/agency, erasure 105–106; inheritance, issue 112; lived experiences 111–112; media bias 105–106; oppression, perceptions 111; support 102

narrative: change 47; expression 139
National Diabetes Prevention Programme, attention 9
NEET, pupil classification 44
nervous system: dysregulation 191, 207; regulation 207, 212–213
networking 83–84; opportunities, inclusivity (importance) 108–109
neuroception, usage 4
neurodivergence 76
neurodiversity 197
neurolinguistic programming (NLP), training 178
Neurosequential Model of Reflective Supervision (Perry) 198, 207
neurotypicality 209
NHS, exit 223
niqab, media bias 106
non-Pakistani Asan men, statements (hurt) 105
nonverbal communication 231
NPQH, uselessness 50

occupational hazards 143
online CBT courses 60–61
ONS study 204
openness, increase 132
oppression: day-to-day experiences 85–86; execution 131; training 120
organisational care 16–17
organisational immune systems, support/buffering 147
organisational stress, workshops/training 143
organisational trauma 138
organisational work, experience 141
organisation culture change, examination 80
organisations: anti-racist practice, embedding 92–93; employment, finding 30; empowerment 23–24; healing 62; help function, improvement 57; kindness, existence 57; leading 50; realities 203
Osagie, Diana (conversation) 40
otherness, image 106

Index

over-responsibility dynamic, management 187–188
overwhelm 203; risk/vulnerability 213
Owen, Lara 200

paid employment, progression route 30
pain, impact 154–155
Pakistan, misunderstandings 111
Palestine, conflict (impact) 109–110
Palestinians: homeland exit requirement (Trump statement) 101; suffering 133–134
parental separation/disputes, impact 57
parent-child attachment relationship 151
parenting, experience 150
parents, unresolved trauma/fears (unconscious absorption) 186
partnership: cornerstone 10; work, usage 16
parts model, usage 189–190
pastoral care systems 42
pathologisation 63
Peer Mentoring (peer mentoring): consideration 29; experience, usage 30; programme 28
Peer Mentor Leads, basis 29–30
peer mentor training, invitation 29
peer support 83–84
people: action, absence (impact) 85; anchoring 35; assimilation, expectation 88; bad experience 227; baggage 45; care, amount 57–58; connection, ability 165; development 67–68; employment, skills/talent (impact) 37; humanness, ensuring 48; interaction 48; power 155; service, reason 43–44; support, providing 34; talk/dialogue, having 49–50; tokenistic action, impact 85; voting process 45; young people, cultural identity/religion/belonging (enhancement) 88–89
perimenopause 205
Perry, Bruce 198, 207
persecution: collective trauma 110; theme 148–149
personal choices, individual preferences (equivalence) 107
personal cost (love) 43
personal experience 179–180; usage 64
personal healing journey, importance 188
personal significance, sense 76
person-centred therapy, usage 61
Peters, Carrie (conversation) 27
phraseology, avoidance 197
physical contact, soothing 233–234
physical education (PE), clothes (wearing) 53
physical exhaustion, perfect storm 206
physical system, support/buffering 147
play therapy 202
point of conflict 45
policymaking, impact 18
political beliefs, differences 239
polyvagal theory (Porges) 206–207; development 4
Polyvagal Theory (Porges) 3
Pope, Alexandra 200, 202

Index

Porges, Stephen 3
Postgraduate Certificate in Education (PGCE), completion 163
poverty of circumstance, presence 53
power: imbalance 238; impact 93; intrinsicness 127; relationships 149–150
powerlessness 155; feeling 152
practice, enhancement 80
practising Muslim/non-practising Muslim, distinction 107
practitioner: experience 78; well-being 221
prayer spaces, allowance 107
pre-colonial practices 120
premenstrual syndrome 207–208
prevention initiatives 10
principles of good supervision (Talking Heads) 228
Priory Hospital, addiction therapy course 179
private narratives, sharing 43
private tutors, absence 42
privilege, relationships 149–150
problems, tackling 43
productivity, increase 119
professional/lived experience, dichotomy 63
professional socialisation 58–59
proper channels, access (impossibility) 132–133
prosody 4
protective factors 10
psychoeducation, integration 182
psychological burnout 6
psychological safety: absence 121, 147; importance 109–110; need 142
psychotherapy 202; lessons 177

public health approaches, advocacy 14
Public Health Consultant Registrar, placement 10
pupilas, NEET classification 44

race: class, intersection 134; systemic irregularities 213; treatment, difference 87; white construct 93
Race Equality Week (REW) 97
racial abuse, impact 87
racial formation: impact 134; sociological theory (Omi/Winant) 118
racial identity 76
racial literacy: absence 134; issues 133
racial microaggression, identification/understanding 124
racial trauma 93; consideration, discomfort 89–90; considerations 94; experiences, impacts 89; impact 81, 84–86, 96; impact, mitigation 127; inequity, discussion 84–85; resistance 90
racism: challenge 88–89, 95, 238; day-to-day experiences 85–86; definition 93; discussion 84–85; focus 134; fueling 105; interpersonal anti-racism 123–124; interpersonal racism, reduction 124; lived experience 94; pervasiveness, witnessing 102–103; presence 186; staff lived experiences 81–82; understanding 124–125
racist ideology, hearing 89
racist policies, impact 76

Index

racist riots, impact 236
Ramadan, respect 110
receptionist, behaviours (impact) 58–59
Red School 202
reflective practice, example 143
reflective reading groups, occurrence 96–97
refugee, children/youth (career involvement) 78–79
Relational Practice Lead, role 117
relationships: core 224; importance 238
relaxed state 4
religion, systemic irregularities 213
religious beliefs: differences 239; impact 94
religious literacy, promotion 109
Research in Practice 81
residential settings, communication 222
resilience, demand 51–52
resources: absence 205; intentional misuse 17
restorative justice 43
right-wing conversations, occurrence 239
risk, understanding 29–30
RJ meeting 43
Rwandan genocide 148

Saad, Layla 83
safeguarding 96, 233; control 171; issue 81; perspective 67; practice/feature 128–129; risk 2023
Safeguarding in the Classroom (Innes-Turnill) 220
safe spaces: creation 95–96; reaction 88–89

safety: feeling, absence 9–192; importance 32; structure support 18
school: attendance 53; external agencies, communication 172; nurse, presence 170; physical education (PE), clothes (wearing) 53; threshold 169–172; thriving, system 44; trip, remembrance 52–53; walking 53
School for Social Entrepreneurs 223–224
seasonal affective disorder 207–208
secondary traumatic stress 203; vulnerabilities 214
Seigal, Dan 237
self-assessment 63–64
self-awareness: ignoring 167; maintenance 209; role 177
self-care: absorption 16–17; consideration 5; consistency 208; practice 17; role modeling, leader effort (importance) 15; toolbox 168
self-compassion 210
self-education, usage 120
self-harm 76
self-leadership, menopause (connection) 200
self-medication 183, 186
self-reflection 123
self-regulating strategies, creation 168
self-story 139
seniority, irrelevance 68
senior leader, behaviour 58–59
senior leadership 167
services: leading 67–68; user feedback/audits, usage 81

Index

sexism, presence 186
sexual abuse 146
sexuality, systemic irregularities 213
shame, feeling 152
shared language, creation 143
shared lived experience, absence (feeling) 34
shared murals/symbols, creation 154
Shohet, Robin 226, 238
Siegel, Dan 207
silence, conspiracy 142
skill set 41
skills, requirement 68
skin colour, derogatory statement (impact) 86–87
slavery 148; consideration 139; legacy 93; perspective 151
social acceptance, requirement 76
social care 197, 206
social, emotional, mental health (SEMH), specialisation 164
social GRACES 149
social media, leader articulation 45
social services, Black/Brown people (interaction) 129
social time, loss 121
social work: assessments 96; career 56–57; practice, development 88; roles, candidates (blind/anonymous shortlisting) 84; training, consideration 66–67
social worker(s): mistrust, reasons 90–91; practitioner/manager experience 78; professional duty 63; responsibility 57
society: division/inequity/discrimination/racism 93; trauma, increase 191

socioeconomic status 76
solidarity, spaces 155; example 142–143
somatic dysregulation 182
Somatic Experiencing (Levine) 207
somatic memory, trauma (embedding) 146–147
somatic system 180
somatic work, integration 182
South Africa, apartheid 149
space. *see* safe spaces: allowance 167; cleaning 69; healing space, opening 144; prayer spaces, allowance 107; thinking spaces, example 143
spirituality, discussion 226
spiritual system, support/buffering 147
staff. *see* Black staff members: burnout 235; complete knowledge, impossibility 59; emotional support, Black psychotherapist (impact) 86; health, reliance 22; interaction 90; investment 61–62; members, engagement/listening events/surveys 83; monthly support groups, setup 83–84; networking 83–84; peer support 83–84; reflective group time 90; room, banter (unimportance) 46–47; social, emotional mental health, well-being (development) 169; support process 62, 84; well-being 230
steel core, origin 44
steeliness, appearance 46

stereotypes: challenge 114; issues 81; lens 88; reflections 94; workforce learning 80
stereotyping: avoidance 107; faith-based stereotyping, avoidance 108
stigmatisation 36–37, 66–67
strategic action plans, development 79
strategic anti-racist lead, employment 79
strategic documents, output 16
strengths-based leadership lens 196
stress 186; cycle, completion 233–234; impact 51–52
stuckness 155
Sturt, Penny 224
success, cornerstones 13–14
suffering, impact 154–155
suicidal ideation 76
supervision: anchor 233–234; discussion 229; ethical accountability 227; importance 220; mandate 226–227; offering 198–199; priority 170–171; quality 225; recommendation 221; regularity 32–33; role 236–237; senior leader engagement 235–236; seven-eyed model 223–224; spirituality, discussion 226; Super Vision, discussions 143
supervisor: listening 230; supervisee, relationship 226–227
support layer, addition 22
support, providing 33–34
survival responses 221
systemic challenges, addressing (importance) 10
systemic devaluation, racist policies (impact) 76
systemic discrimination, display 123–124
systemic oppression 145; consideration 139
system-wide approach 9–11
system-wide effort, absence 11–12
system-wide initiative 10

Tales, Sophie (conversation) 163
talk/dialogue, having 49–50
Talking Heads: formation 223–224; principles of good supervision 228; relationships, maintenance 224; supervisors, training/experience 227
teacher, feedback 153
teaching jobs, presence 45
team, need 47
tension, appearance 168
therapeutic impact 61
therapeutic provision, quality 60–61
therapeutic services 197
therapeutic support, confidentiality (opportunity) 60–61
therapy, discussion 229
thinking spaces, example 143
Thornewood, Tara 223
threat, feeling 152
tick box exercise 79, 145, 191–192; DEI tick box exercise 85
tick box supervision 226
time: intentional misuse 17; volunteering 30
tool kit, usage 169
Torah, misinterpretations 112
toxic masculinity 131
training programme, delivery 28

Index

transference risk 63
trapped, feeling 155
trauma. *see* racial trauma: adaptive responses 181–182; addiction, separation 178; ancestral trauma 138, 148–150; appreciation 58; aspects 185–186, *187*; care 57–58; cause 87; cause, language (usage) 91; commonness 181–182; considerations 138; decolonising, relationship 119; developmental trauma 185; display 141–142; embedding 16; examination 91; experience 32, 166; historical trauma 93, 140; history 4; impact 22, 210; integration 178; intergenerational trauma 77, 93, 138–140, 142, 145; meaning, misunderstanding 181; medical trauma 146; multigenerational trauma 140; psychotherapy lessons 177; response 165, 183; reticence 184; scope 12; staff understanding, development 87; ubiquitous/commonness/prevalence 142; vicarious trauma 6, 198, 203, 213; workshops/training 143
trauma-informed approaches 16, 19, 119; journey 27
trauma-informed care, embedding 18–21
trauma-informed culture 117
trauma-informed framework, historical considerations 133
trauma-informed leadership: embedding 13–14; modelling 7, 14–18
trauma-informed lens, usage 5, 122

trauma-informed organisation, result 17
trauma-informed practice: discussion 86–87, 94; integration 20; principles 120; safety, importance 32; shaping 19; training programme, involvement 28
trauma-informed principles 133; leader integration 13
trauma-informed service system/setting 17–18
trauma-informed settings 164, 220, 235–236
trauma-informed system, approach 8
trauma-informed toolkit, usage 133
trauma-informed universal approaches 146
trauma-informed values, infusing/embedding 144–145
trauma-informed work, excitement 20
trauma-informed workplace culture 144
trauma lens 181; absence, risk 181–182; impact 182–183
traumatic content/experiences 206
Treisman, Karen (conversation) 138, 143
Troubles, the 148
Trump, Donald (DEI cessation executive orders) 101
trust: absence 147; improvement 144–145
Truth and Reconciliation Commission 154

unbelonging system, impact 75
uncomfortable conversations, support 82

Index

unhealed trauma, manifestation 178
University of Exeter 212
USAID, Trump cancellation 101

vagus nerve ("the wanderer"), health/behaviour regulation 4
values: access 141; alignment 173; discussion 45
Venn diagram 229
verbal communication 231
vicarious trauma 6, 198, 203; risk/vulnerability 213
victims, justice: importance 104; support 104–105
violence, root causes 11
Virtual School 197–198
vision: creation/leadership 67–68; enacting 69
voices: absence 76; amplification 21–24
Voyage, The 180–182, 192–193; waves 188
vulnerability, value 236

wages, advance 48
war, impact 148, 236
Weaving a Web of Belonging (Cherry) 75
well-being: creation 130–131; financial investment, requirement 62; hour, offering 33; hubs, reliance 22; increase 119; offer, honesty 56; offer, interrogation (importance) 61; piece 197; planning 24; supervision, relationship 231
western knowledge, privileging 151–152

Weston, Lisa Lea (conversation) 171, 220
West Yorkshire: case, development (initiation) 13; health and care services 23; journey 21
West Yorkshire Health and Care Partnership 11
West Yorkshire Violence Reduction Partnership (WY VRP) 10–11
white, identification 126
whiteness, viewpoint 89
white privilege, financial privilege (conflation) 130
white senior leaders/staff, *Me and My White Supremacy* reading 83
white supremacy, power 94–95
white women, depictions 124
wokeness, responses 152
women, expression (freedom) 103
work: decolonisation, complexity 117; exit 52; lived experience, usage (willingness) 35–36; mistrust/tension 142; purpose/confidence 36; trauma 32
workforce: care, absence (indicator) 58; confidence, building 88–89; demand 231; development, examination 80; focus 230; impacts 28; initiation, reasons 22–23; operational/strategic change, impact 83; supervision support 237; support 81–82; understanding 23
Workforce Race Equality Standard (WRES) 81
work of love, performing 43
workplace: allyship, fostering 111; cultural literacy, fostering 111; decolonising 117; function,

Index

ability 62; interplaying factors 139–140; laughter, presence (importance) 48; love (term), meaning 40–41; psychological safety, absence 121
workshops, delivery 81
workspace, Muslim women (examination) 105–107
world (opening), education (impact) 53

xenophobia: fueling 105; pervasiveness, witnessing 102–103

young people: cultural identity/religion/belonging, enhancement 88–89; outcomes, improvement 232

zero-hour contract, usage 42

For Product Safety Concerns and Information please contact our EU
representative GPSR@taylorandfrancis.com
Taylor & Francis Verlag GmbH, Kaufingerstraße 24, 80331 München, Germany

www.ingramcontent.com/pod-product-compliance
Lightning Source LLC
Chambersburg PA
CBHW071736150426
43191CB00010B/1602